For my son Matthew-Anthony---Thank you for making everything worth it. And for my grandfather Daddy-Jones --Thank you for all the valuable lessons.

Acknowledgements

If someone had told me that I would be writing a story about my life at thirty-one, I would have been skeptical. I'd have doubted I'd have the strength and courage to reveal myself in such a candid way. The easiest thing would have been for me to put on a mask and get into character like we are all taught to do, but I wanted to feel liberated. Liberated from the restraints and boundaries that society has set up for us that often cause us to live in a state of despair and disarray.

On my continuous quest for self-improvement, I am reminded every day how imperfect I am, and how much room for improvement there is in almost every aspect of my life. I embrace it, as I know that as long as we are living, we have to keep working on ourselves. The only thing that is constant is change.

The journey of self-discovery is a continuous one, and as long as we are living, we will continue to discover more about ourselves and why we are here. On my journey, I have been blessed to meet and share my world with some wonderful people who have helped in my quest of self-discovery and improvement, and although this space is too small to thank everyone, to a special few, who have made a huge difference, I would like to say thank you.

To my son Matthew-Anthony, who I am continuing to learn more from every day about what it truly means to be selfless, patient, kind, and loving--- thank you. You are such a beautiful light in the world and in my life, and I am blessed and honored to be your mother. You continue to inspire me to strive to be my best, so I can make you proud. Thank you for being my little angel and for the million kisses daily.

To my mother, Cecilia Saari who remains my constant and greatest role model, I remain in awe of you and continue to be proud to say that I'm your daughter. Thank you for allowing me to spread my wings by never attempting to change me, and allowing me to be a curious butterfly. You have raised my siblings and me with discipline, great values and exemplary leadership, of which I will be eternally grateful. You define the word "mother" in every way, and I hope I can be a great mother to Matthew as you are to us. When I grow up, I'm still hoping to be just like you! (Smile)

To Jonathan Guy-Gladding; my editor, graphic designer and friend. Your commitment, dedication and invaluable contribution to this book is one I am eternally grateful to you for. Thank you for your belief in me, and for encouraging me to speak my truth. You have been a great source of inspiration and strength in my life, and I know that this book would not be possible without you and your incredible insight. Thank you for being my halo.

My sincere thanks to Shirley Gladding for your meticulous proofreading and getting it done in such a timely manner. Thank you for your graciousness and hard work.

A heartfelt thank you to my beautiful siblings whom I love so dearly--- you continue to inspire me in your own unique ways. I am proud to be a sister to you all, and I'm thankful for the wonderful bond that we share which keeps us connected. Thanks for all the great laughs and for keeping me grounded.

A heartfelt thank you also to Mikolaj Sroda for sharing the dream of traveling the world with me. You helped made the world a smaller place for me, and shared in my vision. I will treasure all the wonderful memories on our journey, and will be forever grateful. You will always hold a special place in my heart. Thank you for giving me the greatest gift of all, our son-Matthew-Anthony.

To my best friend, Cardine Alcindor, thank you for fifteen years of wonderful friendship. You've seen me at my highest and lowest, and we continue to weather every storm. Thank you for always supporting me and for being a true friend throughout the years. Most importantly, thank you for being you.

A special thank you to Rodney Belgrave, Jacquelyn Mathurin, Naila Williams, Amanda Charles, Rashid Jn. Baptiste, Valerie Flavien, Ethel Jn. Baptiste, Mary Ubaka, Radhika Rao, Eishnel Henry, Nadia Sebastian Griffith, Tesa Leonce, Paul Fletcher, Caroline Horberg, Caroli Beausoleil, Eric Verdassdonk, and Karen Roberts. Thank you for all your friendship, support, kind words and encouragement throughout the years.

To my beautiful nieces and nephews whom I adore, thank you for inspiring me to be my best so I can be an example to you all. And to all the wonderful and beautiful people whom I have connected with through social networks over the years, and have been ever gracious and kind to me with their wonderful feedback and generous words of encouragement--- thank you. Because of you all, I was able to find the courage to keep pursuing my dream and to be myself. You all inspire me every day to be better and live my best life.

And last but definitely not least, the highest recognition and praise to the almighty for giving me the faith and strength to believe in myself and find the courage to write this book. Without him, nothing is possible, with him, all things are possible. Just look at all what he has done for "A Girl Like Me."

A Girl Like Me

by

Loverly Sheridan

1

The Word "Impossible" Simply Means I´M –Possible!

Growing up on the tiny, beautiful Caribbean island of Saint Lucia, I had quite a vivid imagination, which took me far beyond the small island where I was born and raised. Of course, it often got me into more trouble than I needed. As a child, I often imagined what it was like being on a plane way up in the sky, and if it was possible to stretch my hands out of the window and touch the clouds. I imagined people living in the clouds and wondered if I would be able to see God while I was up there. My greatest wish then was to touch all the ice cream inside the television, which I later learned was snow.

In my dreams, I felt connected to a greater world. A world that transcended race, gender, cultures, religion and age. It was just me in a place with people like me, and many different from me, yet it was the most beautiful chaos that I ever imagined. Over the years, I became the neighborhood pest to visitors coming to the Island from all over the world, and would often bombard them with questions about their homeland. Their varied responses confirmed to me that there was indeed an entire world out there which ignited even more curiosity within me, and a burning desire to learn and know more about this enigmatic world. Back then, it seemed like an impossible dream. I was number four of six children from a single parent household, and the furthest I had ever been was to the south of my island which was one hour away. Those occasional trips for my siblings and me were like a dream coming true. Living in a post-colonial society in the early eighties was challenging. Opportunities to see the world were quite scarce for a girl like me. Most children often become a product of their circumstances, and an understanding of oneself and others was often measured by who they are and what they owned.

At an early age, I understood that life would not be fair to a girl like me. I was a product of a broken home, and according to society and statistics, the chances of me attaining success were minimal. For my mother, trying to survive the harsh realities of life as a single parent was a daily struggle, so the idea of a vacation seemed like a fairytale. However, she seldom complained, and I never felt guilty for being born, nor did I feel like I was a burden to her. She would often boast that motherhood felt as natural to her as breathing. She raised us with class, grace, and with such discipline that although we were poor, I always felt rich. Undoubtedly, there were areas that she struggled with, but somehow she always managed to keep her head and ours above water. My mom is mentioned throughout this book because she has always been and still is a powerful force in my life.

Growing up on an island was great fun. I enjoyed the purities of my childhood and our wonderful cultural traditions and customs. It was great being a part of a community of people where everybody felt like family. In those days, it did take a village to raise a child, and every man or woman was seen as an aunt or uncle. I found good company in the midst of the older folks who always shared great tales of our island. Mr. Fred, the milkman, was one whose company I thoroughly enjoyed. I often sat and waited for him on my door step to accompany him on his farm for his daily routine of feeding the cows. Every day I had a tale of my own to share with him where he would usually burst out into laughter. He would often joke that I was like a "little madam," wise beyond my years. One of the things that brought me the most joy was watching Mr. Fred speak to his cows. I would stand there in amazement wondering if he knew that they could not respond to his questions. The cows would evoke all kinds of emotions from him which I found quite amusing.

My grandfather on my mother's side, "Daddy Jones," was also someone whom I loved to be around. He was a robust and stern man, but he always had a fascinating story to tell. I would sit and listen to his tales of joy and horror, which often left me feeling scared or happy. Daddy Jones played a major role in my life as a child. He was a single parent to my mother from the time she was seven months old, so he was actively involved in our lives and upbringing. Although he was quite strict, his discipline helped foster great values and morals within us, which ultimately shaped me into the woman that I am today. He created a legacy for my family that is rooted in discipline, humility, and love.

On most days on the island, I spent long hot hours playing outside with other children, and running around in open fields being at one with nature. We had few toys, but that did not matter, as we found great pleasure playing with all the natural things from the earth. We used stones to play such games as *"ticky toc,"* and used wood to make skate boards and sling shots, which we called *"catapults."* We also used rope to play *"double dutch and chinese skip,"* and we enjoyed looking for mangoes and other fruits that were in season. I spent most summers in the countryside chasing chickens and watching cows being milked. On rainy days we loved running around chasing each other in our underwear. Every Sunday we looked forward to seeing the man in the white wagon selling local ice cream. Such treats were quite a luxury for us back then.

Night time story telling was always the best, because it usually consisted of stories with "*bolonms* and devils," which always made us scared to fall asleep. My friends and I always feared that a "*bolonm*," (a supernatural character who looks like a child, and makes a crying sound like a cat) would take us away while we slept. Back then, we fell into sleep by candle light or with kerosene lamps since most houses were not yet wired with electricity. I was something of a ring leader, and was often the teacher when my friends and I played school. Not surprisingly, it's a role that stayed with me throughout my life. While I loved the company and interaction of others, I also enjoyed being alone and found that my imagination could take me to places that were far more interesting to me than playing with my friends. Throughout my life, although I've maintained great friendships, I find happiness in solitude and am still amazed at how far my imagination can take me. I had a happy childhood. I was always a happy and cheerful spirit and loved people. I looked forward to weekend getaways with family friends, and whatever adventures that came along the way. I've learned that it really does not take much more than warmth and love for a child to be happy.

Growing up, my dreams of traveling the world seemed like they would remain nothing more than a figment of my imagination, but I always kept them alive. In my heart I believed that one day I would see the world through my own eyes and not through the television. Fast-forward fifteen years and twenty-eight countries later. At the age of twenty four, I started on my journey which now includes thirty countries on six continents. I've visited countries that surpassed my wildest dreams. I've seen some of the most fascinating and enchanting places, and met the most beautiful and interesting people. I've had some life-changing moments and experiences which redefined my purpose and perception of the world, and I quickly learned one important lesson about life- that all the word "impossible" is saying is I´M-POSSIBLE.

2

The American Dream- Not Always What It Seems.

My journey began at the age of eighteen when I migrated from my beautiful homeland of Saint Lucia to the U.S and joined my mother who had been living in Florida for seven years. It was what I deemed the start of the "American Dream." Finally, all my childhood fantasies would come true! It was the beginning of a whole new world, one I had only imagined or seen on television. On our drive home from the airport, I was amazed at how big everything was. The smoothly paved five lane highways seemed like a never ending race car track. It was so different from the narrow, pot holed roads that I had gotten use to in the Caribbean. I had never seen so many different cars in all shapes, colors and sizes.

The tall skyscraper buildings along the highways looked like they could touch the sky, and the big billboards with pictures of celebrities and television programs made me feel like I was in my own movie. One of the things I was looking forward to seeing the most was McDonald's. I had seen it on television and dreamt about what it would be like to go there. On our drive home, I had lost count of how many I'd seen. It was like everything I imagined as a child and had seen on television. In that moment, I realized that dreams do actually come true. As we approached my mother's house, I sat in total awe at the entrance of the community in which she lived. It was a private, exclusive community and we first had to go through security before we could enter. I was captivated by the beauty that surrounded me and couldn't believe that this was my new life. My mom had since married and life had improved significantly for my siblings and me.

When we got through security, I stared in amazement at the large homes with pools and neatly manicured lawns. The community had a golf course, tennis court, gym, and other amenities. Our house was on a peaceful and quiet street with few houses. It was a beautiful home inside and out, and was equipped with beautiful furnishings and wonderful décor. When I entered my mother's closet, it seemed like a store. It was neatly designed with racks of clothes, shoes, handbags and accessories. Her master bedroom was almost the size of the house we lived in back home. That night I took a long, hot shower. In Saint Lucia, we used an outdoor shower to bathe, and sometimes my showers would be abruptly cut short by my frugal grandfather who would close the main pipe to prevent us from wasting water. Some of his antics would infuriate me, like when he would turn off the main electrical switch in the middle of watching a television program to conserve electricity, or shorten all telephone conversations even when someone called us to avoid paying high fees. Today, I find great humor in it all.

    We spent the next few days and weeks discovering new places, and remained in awe of all the beautiful things that surrounded us. I can still remember our first trip to the mall. It was one of the most beautiful places that I had ever seen. There was such a variety of stores, and a wide range of items to choose from. My mom wanted to get us everything we wanted, and she did. It was very hard for her to say no to us. I think she wanted to make up for the seven years that she had spent away from us. I could see the joy in my mom's eyes as she watched our excitement over our new life. There was always something new to discover in the U.S, and the possibilities seemed endless. This is one of the things I love the most about America: no matter who you are, or where you come from, when you get there you have the feeling that anything is possible. You feel alive and want to have bigger dreams for your life. This was a whole new world for me and it was great to be sharing it with my mom. After all the years of hardship that my siblings and I had to endure, it felt like life had taken an incredible turn for the better. It was a much different life than the one we had in Saint Lucia, and I felt very lucky to have it.

    A few weeks later, I started college, and soon after I received my driver's license and was able to drive anywhere I wanted. I loved the freedom and luxury of being able to move around as I pleased. I remembered having to cram my long legs inside small minivans packed with people, goods and produce on hot days with no air conditioning. It felt great being able to enjoy life as a normal teenager in America, and do the little things that I had missed out on in Saint Lucia while my mom was gone. My mom showered us with almost everything we desired and the difficult years we spent apart slowly began to fade. I had settled into my new life and home, and was enjoying a life of endless possibilities. I was certain that all my childhood struggles and problems were behind me, but ironically, they had only just begun.

For a while, I numbed the lingering pain and suffering of my years living away from my mom with material things, and after the novelty wore off, I started to observe people around me differently. My new lifestyle seemed to be moving at a rapid pace, and sometimes it felt overwhelming. I started to realize that people were drawn to me for what they thought I had, and I often felt used. It became increasingly difficult to trust others, rarely was anyone as genuine as they seemed, nor did they keep to their word. My new life was one I always dreamed of having, but once I got it, I started yearning for the simple life that I had left behind in Saint Lucia. Although we didn't have much then, we were happy. Over time, I started feeling stifled by my mother's rules, and unchallenged because everything was being handed to me. I was used to having to care for my siblings and maintain a household, and now I had no responsibilities. There was no joy in getting things easily, and I missed feeling useful and needed. My mother had resumed her role of being a strict disciplinarian, and since I was used to making my own decisions, it was hard to adhere to her rules. After two years of living with her, I decided to move out on my own against her wishes to gain my independence.

The challenges of living on my own, going to college and having a job were a lot more than I anticipated. It didn't take long before I realized that the land of the free wasn't so free. While most people appeared to have been blessed with everything, they were always searching for something more. It seemed like a form of emptiness that constantly needed something or someone to refill it. Most people measured others by what they owned rather that what they stood for. Television talk shows and other programs fed into that need and capitalized on it with sensational programs on celebrities with "perfect" lives, or people who were completely lost. There was hardly any medium or balance. The media loved to build people up, only to tear them down. They were always searching for the next new star to be the beacon of hope or hero to others, meanwhile creating impossible standards for even the celebrities to live up to. Most people wore a brave face and appeared happy, yet inside many seemed to be crying out for help. Optimism impregnated the air, "America, all is possible, and all is well! America, America, where everything is swell." But was it really?

It didn't take long before I got sucked into all the hype. Like everyone else, I wanted it all. I didn't realize back then that the beauty of life at eighteen was in *not* having it all. Today, I observe the youth as they go through life like lightening, only to be at a standstill later on feeling completely lost. I wish someone had told me back then that I had my entire adult life ahead of me which would require me to be responsible and grown up. Our youthful days are the times for trial and error, and to challenge our inhibitions. Conventional living inevitably took hold of me, and by twenty-one, I started aspiring for the material things of the world like everyone else. Meanwhile, everyday seemed like the day before. I was living the fun life of a college student while working part time. I was attending University because I thought I needed to, and I had chosen a major that seemed the most practical, while busily planning for the one size fits all American dream life: husband, kids, career, and home. I was in a relationship with a great guy who was my best friend, but I think we had both reached the stage where we were not sure why to continue it or how to end it. Like most couples, we were at that complacent stage where it's safer to stay than to risk everything and leave, even when you feel like something is missing.

My life seemed mundane and like everyone else's. I was an honor student, yet my brain felt stagnant. Acquiring knowledge meant cramming the content of text books into my head to receive a grade. Rarely did I focus on what I was doing, nor was I gaining any meaningful skills or knowledge that could be utilized in the real world. I was too busy planning for my next task. It seemed like it's almost a prerequisite for most Americans to believe that one should never get too comfortable, and should always be preparing for the next goal or task ahead. I'm sure you're probably thinking that this is the normal, expected life of a young adult and what more could I have possibly wanted from life as a twenty-something, right? It was simple, a sense of purpose! One that was not defined by the acquisitions of "things" and shallow expectations. Something that was greater than the life that I felt had been predesigned for me. One where I did not feel like I was simply existing instead of living. One where I was in the driver's seat of my life.

I was in the land of the "free," yet I did not feel so free. I had everything and more that I felt any young woman needed- a great boyfriend, good job, nice car, nice condo, full closet of clothes and shoes, a good network of friends, and a comfortable life. However, I realized that while I seemed to have it all, my entire life seemed to have been passing me by. My family and friends all had comfortable lives, but I hardly saw them. We were all so busy. I hardly got to drive my nice car because it was always parked in the parking lot at work. I made fairly good money, but it went right to the bank to maintain a lifestyle that in essence I could not afford. I was eating great food, but I wasn't so healthy or in great shape. I had access to an abundance of resources and opportunities, yet time never permitted me to enjoy any of it. I never seemed to have enough time. In the U.S the acquisition of wealth often takes precedence over family and quality time. It always amazes me how taking time off is a luxury for people from the wealthiest country in the world.

At the time that I was questioning the order of things, the U.S had a stable economy, but, only a few years later, many of us would be forced to reevaluate our own lives when the economy took a major down turn. With the sub-prime mortgage fiasco and other economic collapses, many Americans were forced to re-examine their lives and redefine their purpose. Many decided to cut back and began paying more attention to all the waste in their lives. This economic collapse was more than the exposure of the dark side of capitalism; it was a wakeup call for Americans to start owning and taking responsibility for their lives. After five years of living in the U.S with its ups and downs, I had reached a point in my life where I felt a sense of complete emptiness. Somewhere over the course of those five years, I had lost touch with that simple island girl, and became what some might call "Americanized," which suggests among other things being spoilt or having a sense of entitlement. I had replaced the virtues that I was raised with, like humility and gratitude, with pride and self-absorption. There was always a desire for more; nothing ever seemed to be enough. The worst part was that I was denying a big part of myself or who I was to fit into some ideal that I did not even adhere to or believe in. This caused me to question my life and existence. I thought that there had to be more to life than solely earning a college degree, having a husband, children, and having a nice house with the white picket fence.

Although there is nothing wrong with those aspirations, it was apparent to me that because of societal pressures, most people tend to live and think inside of a box, and anyone else with other aspirations seems to be classified as selfish or a failure. I began to wonder, why not first have an understanding of who we are and establish our own lives and sense of self before attempting to raise another life. Most people before the age of thirty feel an overwhelming amount of pressure to have a family, home and career. Often we are torn between either following our own personal ambitions and goals, or trying to fit in, only to end up feeling completely lost, confused and angry in the process. It takes great courage to be true to one self, as an open mind is not something that is often encouraged or embraced.

All these changes from within caused me to reflect on my life, and the voice inside me back when I was a little girl began to speak to me again. I started yearning to see more of the world and what more was out there. We often cannot explain those curiosities and why we need to fulfill them, we just know that we have to. I loved America, and was grateful for the opportunities that it provided, but I wanted to define my own life. I was tired of competing and aspiring to be like everyone else, even when I was perfectly ok with just being me. I was tired of having to feel like I had to prove myself over and over again, and I was especially tired of denying my own voice to simply fit in. What is the purpose of uniqueness if the world is constantly trying to make us into the image of everyone else? Deep down, I believed that there was more to life and much more to discover.

After a short vacation to England and Ireland while in college, I started to question my life and purpose even more. I liked the collectiveness and simplicity of European culture. When I returned to the U.S, I had an even bigger desire to see more of the world. I wasn't sure what I was searching for, but I knew that there was something more to discover on my journey, and I needed to find out what it was. Some may argue that I was lost, but I think I was simply *searching,* and would keep searching until I found what I was looking for. We are all on a journey of self-discovery; it seemed mine had only just begun.

3

Faith Is Not Knowing, But Doing It Anyway.

During a short visit with my good friend Rashid Jn Baptiste who was living in North Carolina at the time, a conversation with him confirmed to me that I had to make my dreams a reality. Rashid had recently graduated from university and was working for Microsoft. One evening, while at dinner with another friend who had accompanied me on the trip; we started having a discussion on arranged marriages. Rashid was preparing to attend the wedding of one of his colleagues from India whose marriage was arranged. My friend and I had strong opinions about the issue and we spoke vehemently about it. I believe that our closed-mindedness and strong opinions on the matter with little understanding about it frustrated Rashid. He turned and said something to me that caused me to question myself. He said, "I think both of you need to broaden your horizons and step out of your comfort zones. You both need to have more of an open mind, and instead of judging others, get to know them better. Loverly, I think you should look into doing some exchange programs abroad to broaden your views and perspectives of the world." His words resonated with me. Rashid was like a brother and mentor in my life. I looked up to him and admired him, so his opinion meant a great deal to me.

I remembered his words, and thought of ways in which I could begin my journey. The opportunity never presented itself, but the thought was never far from my mind. One day, during my finally semester of college, while contemplating what I wanted to do with the rest of my life, I decided that this would probably be the best time to pursue a Master's Degree in another country. It was only a few months before graduation and I wanted to start a Master's program right away. It seemed impossible, as time seemed against me. I also did not have the required funds and I didn't know where and how to get started. Nothing seemed to be going in my favor. I approached my guidance counselor with the idea, and her response was discouraging and pessimistic. I decided to do some research of my own online. The country of Australia kept popping into in my mind. I decided to direct all my focus toward it. I believe that the random thoughts in our heads are our own personal psychics, and if we listen to them and act, then we will be amazed at what we discover.

The country of Australia was very appealing to me because it seemed like an entirely different world. It was very far away, and no one I knew had ever been. I had never met an Australian, and knew very little about the country. In fact, the only thing I knew about Australia was that there were many kangaroos. Since I am a curious butterfly and I'm always seeking to challenge myself, I decided that this country would be perfect for me to pursue a Master's Degree in International Relations. I applied to three Universities online, and amazingly I got accepted into all three. Funding was my biggest issue. A Masters education is very expensive. How would I be able to afford this? Through my research online, I learned that financial aid was provided to many universities abroad, and my school was on the list. I quickly applied and was approved! Everything happened right in the nick of time. One of the stipulations for receiving financial aid is that the funds wouldn't be available until school began, so there would be a few weeks during which I would have to survive without that money, but with or without funds I was going. Although my mom was always willing and ready to assist financially, I wanted to maintain my independence and be responsible for my own life. I was a young adult, and I believe that I needed to act accordingly. My attitude towards life challenges and situations are always one of optimism and faith. Two traits mirrored from my mother.

My mother took great risks long before I started on my journey. She had taken the first step by giving up her career as a school administrator to pursue a better life for us in the U.S It was not an easy decision, as she was forced to leave her six children behind. It was necessary however, as life in Saint Lucia was becoming increasingly difficult for her as a single parent. Sacrifices had to be made, and we all had to endure a lot while she was gone, including losing our home and all our belongings during a storm. This inevitably meant that our family had to be divided, and for some time we all lived in different places. This was hard for us, because even if we never had much, we always had our mom and each other, and overnight everything seemed to have fallen apart. After one year of living apart, we moved into a tiny wooden house belonging to our grandfather in one of the roughest areas of Saint Lucia. This was yet another major adjustment, as prior to our mom leaving for the U.S we lived in a middle class neighborhood.

At the age of fifteen, I now had to be the head of household and primary caretaker for two brothers and a younger sister for a few years. It seemed like the responsible thing to do since I was the eldest available sibling and my mom was gone. I didn't realize it at the time, but this experience would shape and define my entire existence. I was forced to grow up quickly and felt the pressure to be responsible at an early age. This probably explains why most of my friends refer to me as an "ole soul," because I've always taken life very seriously and been mature in attitude. This experience instilled in me strength and courage to deal with the many challenges throughout my life. Thankfully, my mom was always very involved in our lives even though she was far away. She guided me every step of the way as best she could on how to handle situations and manage money.

There were times when I felt like I was missing out on my teenage years, especially when my friends were doing all the fun things that teenagers do, like going to parties and road trips around the island, but later on I would learn that sometimes disappointments are really blessings in disguise, and those challenges were preparing me for a world that would require me to have the qualities needed for my journey and survival. It is something that I am extremely grateful for. My mom's decision to make that first step and take such a big chance speaks of her strength and courage. Her decision paved the way for endless possibilities for my siblings and me. I am not sure where I would be today had she stayed in Saint Lucia, but what I do know is that I'm here, and it's a place in which I am happy and comfortable. Some may argue that it was too big a risk for her to leave us behind, and may even judge and condemn her for it, but I don't. I admire her strength and courage to have made such a difficult decision. I've learned that sometimes to get to heaven one first has to go through hell and out of pain come great power.

It is said that we are the sum of all our experiences, and how we respond to them will determine our fate. I believe that everything comes at a price, including life. The price we pay for life is that at some point, we will all have to suffer and eventually die. Such complicated decisions like the one my mother made contributed to my open-minded approach to life and others. It also caused me to question convention in regards to family. Not everything is black and white, nor is it as simple as it may seem. Not all causes have the same effect either. Some children would probably have crumbled under such circumstances, but we didn't, and I think that's primarily because my mom raised us in the church and taught us about God. We prayed and worshipped together as a family, and my mother would always draw reference to God in all things. One of the greatest gifts that my mother ever gave me was teaching me about the Bible and God. Growing up, no matter what I endured, and even now, I have great faith that every experience, good and bad, is usually a blessing in disguise and is directed to teach me something about myself and others. When I mentioned the news to my mom that I was planning on attending school in Australia, I can still remember her reaction. She said, "Oh wow, that's great!" I was just reading a book about it, it's a beautiful place." That's one of the things I love about my mom. She is not a "dream killer," and she did not raise me to be scared of discovering new things.

Everything seemed possible in her eyes, and a seemingly insurmountable obstacle was just another challenge. Because of this attitude and her willingness to take calculated risks to help herself and her family, she is my greatest role model. Most parents would have probably had a million concerns and questions, but my mother was never one to be worried about the little details. She always had faith in my decisions and felt that I was capable of taking care of myself and making good choices. She always encouraged me to listen to my own voice. My friends thought of me as fearless. I was always ready to take on a new challenge, or do things that most would think twice about. In college, I was the girl who drove her car on faith when my tank was without fuel, knowing that it would get me to my destination. I was the girl who didn't know how I would pay my tuition after dropping out of college and losing my scholarship, but signed up for classes anyway. I was the girl who dropped out of college against my mom's wishes to work and be independent. Although I eventually returned to complete my degree, the experience and lessons learned were invaluable.

While most of my friends were probably smarter, richer,

more beautiful, and even more talented than me, I realized back then that there was one thing that worked in my favor; I was not afraid of the unknown. It's important for most parents to remember that they are the window to the world for their child, and how they see it, perceive it and react to it will have a great influence on their child's approach to it also. As parents, we should try not to allow our own fears, failures, insecurities and disappointments to influence or kill our child's dreams, or to place pressure on them. I use the word "try" because I am now a mother, and I know that it is often easier said than done, but the rewards can be greater. Children will eventually grow up and do the things that they want to do anyway. They have minds of their own, so we are better off being a guide than missing out on the journey.

My perception of the world through my mother's eyes was that anything was possible and nothing great can be achieved without taking a chance. At twenty-four, after completing my bachelor's degree in Communications and Women's Studies, which took what seemed like a lifetime to complete, and enduring what seemed like another lifetime of trials and tribulations and many tests, I thought it was the right time for me to broaden my horizons and start living out my dreams. With little money, and a broken heart, since my relationship of two years had also come to an end, leaving me feeling a bit betrayed and angry, I embarked on my journey. It was the first time that I would be living in a country outside of the U.S other than my homeland and Barbados. I wasn't sure what to expect, but I had this calm, reassuring feeling that it would change my life.

4

It's A Small World After All.

I was not sure what to expect from Australia. Everyone I questioned about it had great things to say, and based upon what I read, it sounded like heaven on earth. I imagined a place quite similar to the U.S, but with more vast, wide open spaces. One of the things that I was really excited about was seeing an aborigine in person. I had read a lot about them and thought they were fascinating. I later learned that most aborigines lived in isolated areas, and I probably would not see many of them in the city of Brisbane where I would be living. It did take a few months before I saw any in person.

The flight to Australia seemed like an eternity. It took fourteen hours direct from California. I slept for about ten hours, and was awake for the final four. Upon arrival at the airport, I got my first passport interrogation. I had a Saint Lucian passport at the time which made interrogations routine on my travels. I remember the immigration officer putting in several codes, but nothing came up. He then pulled out a map to see its exact location, or maybe to see if it even existed! Yes! A custom officer did ask me once if the country of Saint Lucia existed! Growing up, the older folks always said that our island was like a dot on the map, but I didn't think that in 2005 it would be so difficult to locate. One of the fascinating things I learned on my journey is how small my island really is, and how much of a "dot" we are in the world. Yet, it's a dot with a unique culture, with some of the most beautiful people, including two Nobel laureates. Not bad for a dot on the map!

Once I got through the interrogation from the immigration officer, I got a huge "Welcome mate" greeting, and the sound of his Aussie accent, along with his beautiful features had me smiling from ear to ear. I couldn't wait to discover my new home! When I arrived at the airport lounge, I realized how clean the surroundings were, but once I got outside it felt like I had entered a sauna. It was hot! Quite surprising for January I thought, but it was summertime in Australia, which explained the humidity. Outside looked clean and beautiful, and everything was very modern. Not the vast, animal kingdom teeming with nature that I was expecting. I took a taxi to my new home which I had arranged via the internet prior to coming. I exchanged emails with a young lady who was looking for a roommate and it seemed like it would work perfectly for us. When I arrived at the apartment, she greeted me with a big smile and a hug, and although she had that warm, easy going, Aussie nature, I knew instantly that it would only be a temporary residence. Her apartment was not the cleanest and she had two cats! I must have missed that in the emails. I love cats, but I can't live with them. We exchanged a few words where she briefed me on a few things, and then she returned to work. It was right before lunch.

I stepped outside to observe my surroundings. It was a nice, quiet, suburban neighborhood. A bit too quiet and it felt like the ground would shake at the drop of a pin. There wasn't a single person in sight, and in that moment, I felt a lot more fragile than I thought. I started questioning my decision, wondering if I had done the right thing. My mind began to wonder. I thought of my ex-boyfriend and how bad things had ended between us. We were best friends, and it was a relationship of love and respect, but we were both graduating from college, was at transitional stages, and feeling the pressures of having to be responsible for someone else's happiness. We felt stifled, but we did not know how to communicate that to each other in an effective way for fear of hurting each other's feelings. Looking back, I can see how my own selfish nature could have caused him to be cold and distant. I had made up my mind to move to Australia and leave everything behind, and I don't think that I articulated my reasons to him very well. I am not sure that I would have been able to even if I tried. *I* was searching for the reason also.

In our relationship, I had taken on the role of "mother" as it was all I had ever known from having to grow up quickly. Learned behavior is a very hard habit to break. I overwhelmed myself and him at times with my take charge, motherly attitude. I didn't know better then, but with time and experience I was able to conceptualize it all. Perhaps, confusion is necessary, as out of chaos usually comes order. In that moment standing outside in the blazing heat, none if it made any sense to me. All I knew was that I was heartbroken and felt betrayed. I wish I had the understanding of things then as I do now, it would have saved me many sleepless nights. After reminiscing, I went back inside, lay on my bed and cried myself to sleep. It was one of the longest days for me. I slept for a few hours, and when I woke up, because of the time difference it was time to sleep again. It felt like a never ending day. My new roommate had gone to bed, and I walked around the apartment in circles being shadowed by her black cat while wondering what I could do to pass the time. I did not have a telephone as yet and there was no internet. It seemed like the longest night. It took a long time before I fell back into sleep. I decided to lie on my bed and read some cards friends had given me at my farewell party. It kept me calm.

Finally, the sun came up and it was a new day! The sun was blazing hot like the day before and I was anxious to get on a bus and explore the city. Australia has a special heat, and some often joke that the reason is because it's the closest to the sun. My roommate gave me the bus information, and I was off to explore the city. Everything seemed so clean and perfectly organized. It was not very crowded, and to my amazement there were many Asians. I imagined that everyone would look like the famous Aussie actor Russell Crowe and actress Nicole Kidman. I later learned that the Asian population is one of the largest groups of people living in Australia and grows rapidly each year. I went to my University to get things sorted out for school, and was amazed by the diversity. There were Australians, Asians, Africans, Europeans, Americans and other groups of people. It dawned on me that rarely in any single place in the world is there any one group of people. We are curious beings, and we continue to move around like Vikings. It was exciting for me to be in the midst of such a diverse population. I knew instantly that the most valuable education I would receive would be outside the classroom.

I spent my first day of school running around getting things organized and did not pay any particular attention to making friends. However, everyone seemed very friendly and helpful. The first impression I got about Australia was that it is a very safe and peaceful place. Everything was in order at my University, and I felt relaxed and comfortable. On my way home to get the bus, I met a young woman from South Africa, she introduced herself and we spoke for some time. I was really excited about this encounter as I had never met anyone from South Africa before. I took this opportunity to tell her about my love and admiration for my hero

Nelson Mandela. At the time I had just bought his book, "A Long Walk to Freedom," and was really captivated with him and his story. Although I had heard and read a lot about him, it was only when I began reading his book that I gained a greater understanding of how special he is. His book and story would ultimately have a great impact on my life.

    As time went by, I settled into my new home and was able to make my way around easily. Within two weeks, I realized that where I lived was located too far from my university, so I found a new place closer to my school. I shared an eight bedroom flat with eight people from various countries. This assigned living arrangement was quite common in Australia and one I enjoyed. While everyone was always busy with their individual lives, there were nights when we gathered with other friends from school, and had wonderful barbeques and dinner nights with great conversation. It gave me the chance to make friends and I got close to a few people. I was beginning to learn new things about myself, like how ignorant I was about the world and the people whom I shared it. Every night I went to bed a little more knowledgeable than the day before. Yet, a part of me felt completely robbed. I felt like there was an entire world out there with so many fascinating places and people, and I questioned myself as to why it took me so long to explore it.

    I was still fairly young, but there were many students who were much younger who spoke about internships in Europe and volunteer work in Africa and Asia, and here I was reaching for a map for every new person I met. This ignorance simply increased my thirst for wanting to learn and know more about the world. I wish life had shown me back then that my value was not determined by the things I owned and that spending all my time trying to grow up too fast and prove my worth through material possessions was doing me more harm than good. In essence, it was blinding me from my inner greatness and realizing my true self.

When I was in a group with my peers from all over the world, they didn't care about the price of my clothes or what brand I wore, as seemed to have been the focus of most of my peers back in the U.S. They were thirsty for knowledge of any kind, and were curious about me, my views, and my perception of the world. This was unfamiliar territory for me, but it felt really good. I was tapping into a new level of self-awareness. I was thinking in ways I never had before. I felt like a new part of me was being born, or reborn. I believe that the humble, simple girl was always there, she was just pushed to the side for the sake of conformity.

5

Life Is Only A Loan, Step Out Of Your Comfort Zone.

When I decided to pursue a Master's degree in International Relations, I thought it would complement my degree in communications and enrich my knowledge of the world and its cultures. I also thought it would provide opportunities in the field of diplomacy in which I was interested. Although I did not have a background in international relations, I believed that the courses that I had previously taken in political science would be helpful. On the first day of my program, I knew that I was in for a challenge. It was a diverse group of students from all over the world, and based upon our first discussion, I realized how advanced everyone was in the subject. They were using terminology and speaking in political terms that I was not familiar with, which was a bit intimidating for me, and once again I doubted myself. Had I made the right decision? Should I have gone the safe route and pursued a master's degree in communications? After all, it was what I was familiar with and quite good at, so why should I humiliate myself in a field that I clearly knew little about?

In our first seminar, I felt like I had learned more about the world than in all my years living. For the first time, I was learning about countries like Dubai and its rapid growth and expansion. I learned more about the history and political divide in North and South Korea of which I had little prior knowledge. I also became more informed about the Israeli and Palestinian conflict, and the new challenges with the Muslim world. All this in one seminar! At the end of the discussion I felt enlightened, but also completely overwhelmed. Everyone was contributing to the discussions and had thought provoking opinions, while I was still trying to grasp the basic terminology and concepts. I felt like a dry sponge just wanting to absorb everything. I was more curious than ever, and I wanted to learn more. It was all a bit humbling; but I believe that there is beauty in not knowing. When we don't know, we tend to approach things with an open mind, and without preconceived notions.

I knew that I would have to put in a lot more work than others because of my lack of knowledge in international relations, but I was ready for the challenge. Since international relations is an ever changing field, I was always enthusiastic about going to seminars and working with my groups. Sometimes the debates were very heated. In 2005, one of the ongoing debates was the tragedy of September 11. Although I was not an American citizen at the time, I had lived in the U.S. for the previous five years, and I did consider it my home. Sometimes it was uncomfortable listening to some of the harsh and even hateful remarks from my peers, but it was yet another eye opening experience for me. I had no idea how the rest of the world viewed the U.S until I got out side of it. I thought everyone loved the USA and wanted to live there, but I was in for a rude awakening.

Although most students shared the same sentiments as I did of September 11- that it was a cowardly and vicious attack on innocent civilians and a crime against humanity, they also had strong opinions about why the attacks took place. In their opinions, America instigated those attacks by invading other countries and interfering with their order of things. I was amazed at how my peers tried to justify the cause of the attacks, more than the act itself. Were they happy that it happened? Gandhi's quote kept playing my head, "An eye for an eye, will make the world blind." It sure felt like the whole world had gone blind. Were they missing the point, that human rights and freedom were in jeopardy, and that anyone of us could be next? It didn't matter what had ignited those attacks, the fact remained that more than two thousand innocent people were dead, and human safety seemed to be imperil. Most of their arguments infuriated me. It even caused me to distance myself from some of them for what I deemed at the time as extreme and hateful views. It was of great concern to me that people who were all pursuing careers in a field that requires the highest level of tolerance were consumed with so much anger and contempt. Most times I felt like I was pursuing a degree in "defending Anti-Americanization."

Today, although my views still remain the same on many points, I think that my attitude toward my peers is different. With time and experience, I've learned to understand that thinking objectively doesn't mean that you will always agree with someone's opinions or understand them. It means learning to think with an open mind and to being respectful of the opinions of others. I believe that in matters of politics and global governance, one does themselves a great disservice by refusing to think objectively or with an open mind. Occasionally an incident occurs which gives me a better perspective on the reasons my peers shared some of the views they had back then. Recently, a black man from Georgia named Troy Davis in the United States was executed. This story had become a global phenomenon since new evidence showed that there were reasonable doubts that he was guilty of the crime for which he was convicted for. Even with heavy protests and thousands of appeals from leaders and even from the Pope, he was executed. A few months prior to his execution, a white young woman named Casey Anthony was accused of killing her five year old daughter. There was overwhelming circumstantial evidence against her, but because a juror found reasonable doubt, she was found not guilty and released. It was another case that shook the nation.

These two cases highlight the contradictions of the American legal system, and continue to divide the masses and fuel the ongoing debate on racism. It also makes it increasingly difficult for loyal citizens to defend our insistence on universal human rights when sometimes we refuse to practice what we preach. Such contradictions often cause the world to view us as hypocrites who refuse to lead by example. I believe that when the principles and values of the most powerful country in the world are not practiced, it sets a dangerous precedent for others to follow. As the leader of the free world, what we need to do is practice what we preach.

6

Greatness Lives In You! People Can Enhance Or Dim That Greatness, But No One Can Give It to You, Or Take it away. Believe In Yourself!

My life in Australia had become routine and it started to feel like my second home. School took up most of my time, since a lot of reading was required and there were quite a few seminars. I had gotten over my fear of not being able to keep up with my peers. International Relations is a very broad subject so we were able to focus on a specific area of study which took away most of my anxiety. However, there was a wide range of topics to cover, and we were expected to have an understanding of its historical context in order to understand contemporary issues. This proved to be especially difficult for me as a lot of it entailed European history, African history, Asian history and American history, none of which I was well versed on. I attended secondary school in the Caribbean where the focus was more on Caribbean history and a little bit of European history which mainly dealt with our mother country Great Britain. Yet, I welcomed the new challenge as it gave me a broader and wider perspective of the world and other cultures.

I became fascinated with African history. What I learned of its breath and complexity spoke volumes to me about the resilience of its people. Their struggles and survival from the depths of slavery and colonialism is a true testament of the power of the human spirit. In essence, learning more about African history gave me a greater sense of pride and understanding of who I am, and where I come from. Many questions remain unanswered, but having some answers is better than total ignorance. One really can't understand where they're going if they don't know where they're coming from. I was beginning to understand the reason for my sense of dislocation for most of my life. They say that knowledge is power, but the more I learned, the weaker I felt. Based upon what I had heard or seen on television, it always seemed like Africa was a poverty stricken continent that continually had to be saved by the West and other wealthy countries. Studying African history made me realize that the wealthy countries are often simply giving back what they had unjustly taken away centuries before.

At school, the debates and discussions were always very interesting. I learned a lot from my peers and got an opportunity to see how they viewed the world. I also was made to question my own perceptions, prejudices and opinions, which were influenced by what I had been taught or told growing up. The easiest thing would have been for me to remain within that mind set and convince myself that I was right, and that my way of seeing and doing things was the right way. However, I realized that I would be selling myself short by denying what I knew was the truth. With each passing day, I found myself thinking more objectively and with a more open mind. I took great pride in silence and in listening. "Knowledge speaks, wisdom listens." As much as I loved discussions and debates, I wished that I didn't have to speak, but could just listen.

As part of our program, we were supposed to make individual presentations. I always loved making presentations and speaking in front of people, but I felt completely intimidated in this setting. It was intense, and my peers were quite critical and seemed to love debate for its own sake. For one of my very first presentations, I thought that my beautiful slideshow of pictures would be enough to overshadow the little content and in-depth knowledge I had on the topic I was presenting. I got a rude awakening and was grilled by my peers. It was something that I was totally unprepared for. I remember going home feeling completely embarrassed and wanting to quit. I was thinking that perhaps this wasn't the right field for me, and that there was no way I would be able to survive another round of harsh criticisms and tough questions. Yet, something greater than me wouldn't allow me to quit. I was determined to be that dynamic presenter that I was capable of being for my next presentation.

I prepared myself day and night and practiced my question and answer session in front of the mirror. I started to think of the opposite side to my argument and found responses that could support that argument. I felt confident that I would deliver effectively this time around, and I did. At the end of the presentation, my professor said one line to me that stuck with me to this day. He said, "Your future is so bright, it's burning my eyes." His words stuck with me throughout my journey, and gave me a sense of confidence that I didn't have before. I realized then the impact of words and positive reinforcement can have on people's lives and how much it can empower them.

7

A Child Will Often Live Up To Whatever You Expect Of Him.

As a teenager, I rarely got any positive feedback from others. When my mom left for the U.S, school became secondary to me, and I lost focus on my school work. Teachers always seemed to highlight the areas that I was weak in, and some saw me as somewhat of a nuisance when I spoke out. Back then, I always believed that I had something important to say, and felt like I was smart. I was wishing someone would take me under their wing and believe in me. However, most teachers rarely had the time to nurture and mentor children. They often seemed stressed and angry. Looking back, I can imagine that working under some of the conditions that they did, probably didn't allow for much of that. Most times, all I wanted was some of the much needed attention that was missing from my life. My mom was gone, my father was absent, and I was essentially raising myself.

My primary and secondary school days were not the happiest times of my life. I believe that the entire structure and design of the school system in my homeland and the Caribbean in general had a great influence on my academic performance. Children are placed in a school based upon a standardized test score from a general examination called Common Entrance Exams. Often, most of the schools comes with labels that instantly place children within a certain hierarchy or bracket that makes them feel either substandard, mediocre, good, better, or great. One of the great harms of colonialism is that long after its demise, its practices and customs linger on and continue to marginalize and divide people. Sadly, it's so entrenched in our psyche and history that although we are an independent nation, we often continue to live in a colonized and dependent state of mind. We raise and teach our children to "emancipate themselves from mental slavery," yet we maintain the same institutions and structures on which these practices were founded. How can we ever truly be free if we don't let go and redefine the systems that were placed to divide us?

I believe a child will live up to (or down to) whatever you

expect of him, and since most expectations for me and others like me were mediocre or negative, I fell through the cracks. I did not take my school work seriously, and found it difficult to remain focused. My test scores at the time placed me in one of the lowest ranked schools on the island, and I believe I lived up to the expectations of the system, my teachers and my peers. However, there was a teacher named Karen Bourne who was the opposite of what many teachers were and had a positive influence on my life and approach to learning. She taught me literature, which became one of my favorite subjects and I always looked forward to her class. She welcomed my opinions and made me feel like I mattered. She seemed to love teaching and was passionate about literature. She taught us with such passion and got really involved with the characters. One of my favorite books from her class was "A Man for All Seasons."

For some reason, this book resonated with me. I loved the story of Sir Thomas More and the role he played. I loved what he stood for and what he died for, and his unwillingness to compromise himself. He risked it all for his beliefs and stayed true to himself at all costs. The world does not need another celebrity or big star, what the world needs is more Sir Thomas Mores. It needs more men and women of leadership and conviction who are willing to die for a cause that they believe in. One of Ms. Bourne's favorite lines when teaching was to "always read between the lines." She constantly reminded us that not everything would be written out for the reader, and that sometimes we have to look beyond what is written and read between the lines. I took this advice with me beyond literature, and applied it to life as well. Ms. Bourne played an instrumental role in me realizing my passion for writing as a child. In her class, I found a safe haven and a voice.

It was not until I moved to the U.S and started University that I began to receive positive feedback from teachers about my abilities. It was there that I realized that it was possible for me to attain a tertiary education and that I was capable of accomplishing anything that I set my mind to. The learning environment at my college was a pleasant one. It seemed that everyone working in that college loved what they did. It was a pleasure going to school every day. They made learning fun, and did not make it seem like a chore. Perhaps, it worked against me later on, as sometimes I did not feel challenged and would feel like I was wasting my time. However, as many times as I failed or repeated a class, I was still allowed to continue my education until completion. Such opportunities are not so readily available in my homeland.

In Saint Lucia and the Caribbean, the opportunities for obtaining tertiary education are quite scarce. Although I had passed all but one of my CXC subjects, I could not go on to the local community college. It was quite competitive, and a lack of resources meant that only the best students could attend. The only option left for me and others like me was to find employment, and jobs were not easy to find. For those whose parents were fortunate enough, they are sent to school abroad. This was not an option for a girl like me back then. Thankfully, my mom had gotten married since moving to the U.S, and was in a better position financially, so one year after finishing high school, she was able to send me to a school on the neighboring island of Barbados for one year to study airline procedures. At the time I was pursuing a career as a travel agent/air hostess as a way to fulfill my dream of traveling the world. As luck would have it, I was studying to be a travel agent at the same time that the internet was exploding. Almost overnight, it seemed, everyone started booking their travel plans online, and travel agents became virtually obsolete. Finding a job as an air hostess also proved to be difficult. It was yet another disappointment for me and I thought that my dreams were slowly dying. However, it turned out to be yet another blessing in disguise. Soon after I moved to the U.S, I enrolled in college, which was possibly the best decision that I've ever made, even if I wrestled with it throughout.

8

We Will Never Know and Understand Each other, If We Are Busy Judging Each other.

The city of Brisbane where I lived in Australia is a beautiful, quiet city in the state of Queensland. It reminded me of the West Palm Beach area where I lived in Florida. Brisbane is tranquil place with lovely beaches surrounded by small suburban communities. I felt safe there, but it was a lot more laid back than I anticipated. I felt like something that I had hoped to find in Australia was missing, but i didn't know exactly what it was. Later, especially after traveling through Europe, I realized that it was a lack of culture. Australia's history and culture is fairly new, making it feel very contemporary compared to Europe which has a distinctly ancient feel. Apart from their colorful accents, I found Australia's culture to be greatly influenced by the U.S. I also found Australians to be generally laid back, easy going people, and quite affable.

One of my closest friends while there was my Aussie roommate Leah. She was an easy going young lady who had this beautiful light about her, which always seemed to brighten anyone's day. I spent many nights talking her to sleep with my random thoughts and countless stories. I can still remember her loud and infectious laugh, and the moments when she would bury her face in her hands when I said something startling. She was curious to learn about me, as I was curious to learn about her. Although she was much younger, she was quite mature in her thinking and her words will always resonate with me. She remained one of my closest friends while in Australia, and we've maintained our friendship ever since. While most Australians were friendly and easy going, some also seemed uninformed on many issues, especially geography. Those that I spoke to had very little knowledge of the Caribbean or the outside world, for that matter. Some thought Jamaica was the only island in the Caribbean. Some asked if Saint Lucia was close to Europe. One guy asked me if there were roads and cars there. A young woman asked me once, "Are you a princess or something? You must be since you are able to come all the way here for school!"

She assumed that the island was so poor that the only way I could afford to have left was because I was a princess or someone very wealthy.

My African, Indian and Chinese friends also had similar questions asked by others with some of the same misconceptions. Some of the questions and comments were mind boggling, which made me realize that ignorance does not discriminate. Initially, I was being hard on myself thinking that my lack of knowledge about the world was because of my geographical location and being from a third world country. However, even in a first world country, most people were equally, if not more ignorant than I was. The misconceptions that some of my classmates had are not necessarily unreasonable because there are still third world and poverty stricken countries in the world, but in every country there are rich and poor people. I've learned it is important when we inquire about people and places; that we ask questions with an open mind. Not everyone from the East is poor, and not everyone from the West is rich either. The catastrophe of hurricane Katrina in the U.S back in 2005 illustrated that point and provided another topic for heated debates in my seminars. My peers could not believe the response to such a major catastrophe by the U.S government. One of the great lessons from Hurricane Katrina was that poverty is often right in our own back yards, yet we look down on others. Through the yawning gaps in geographical knowledge of the many people I met, I was beginning to see how much the world is stereotyped. We know it is wrong to stereotype people because of where they are from, but sadly it´s a reoccurring theme in our world.

We all endeavor to distinguish ourselves and carve out our own identity, but when we are lumped into one large group simply because of where we are from, we feel dehumanized. Back in Florida, many of my friends from Haiti were treated like refugees even though they came from middle class and wealthy families. I believe that no one, despite class or status should have to explain who they are to be treated fairly and with respect. The lack of understanding and awareness among my peers towards each other made me realize that sometimes our misconceptions can really stem from simple ignorance. Most of us genuinely do not know any better. Ironically, there is so much that we don´t know about each other, yet we judge, condemn and hate. Perhaps if we took a little time to educate ourselves and learn more about other people and cultures, then we would understand that being different is not necessarily bad or wrong. It is our differences that add so much beauty to this fascinating world. If we are living in the information age, then what excuses do any of us have to remain ignorant?

9

We Are The Victims Of Nothing And The Survivors Of Everything.

My budget was rather limited while in school, and since I was unable to work because of a demanding class schedule, I didn't get to do as much exploring around Australia as I would have liked. However, I did go on quite a few field trips with friends, and did many fun activities, which usually included food, drinks and music. There was some partying also, where things sometimes got a little wild. At some parties there were people doing drugs and getting high right in front of me. I was amazed at how common it was. I've always gotten high off of life and music and never felt the need to try any drugs, but I tried not to judge anyone who did either. While some of my schoolmates did try drugs, I never did, and I didn't feel like I missed out on anything. One night at a party, one guy tried to get me to participate but I insisted that I would not. He started screaming profanities at me really loud and was acting crazy. I decided the best thing would be for me to leave, and I did. I often wonder how different my life might have been had I tried it just once. Perhaps it wouldn't have changed anything, but perhaps it would have. There are certain risks that I am just not willing to take.

As a child, I had seen or known of drug addicts and alcoholics from my neighborhood, but I had never experienced seeing drugs done right in front of me. I think seeing that made me want to be even more in control of the situation around me by remaining sober and keeping a clear mind, even if everyone seemed to be losing theirs. It goes to show that being in the presence of something doesn't necessarily mean that you are obliged to do it also, or that you are an advocate for it. People are going to do what they want to do, with or without your approval, but it's important to stay true to yourself and not allow yourself to be influenced by your peers simply because you don't want to stand out. You may not be liked or become popular for it, but you will eventually earn respect. I am thankful that my mother never shielded me from the harsh realities of the world. Instead, she always told us about it and the damage that it could cause. She loved sharing the experiences of others with us so we could understand some of the realities of life.

One of the things I thoroughly enjoyed doing everyday while in Australia was going for my long walks. It really helped clear my mind and I especially loved being outdoors. Australia is a beautiful, clean country, so those walks were always a pleasure. I looked forward to them every day, and they always helped me to feel rejuvenated and remain focused. Although months had passed, I was still somewhat angry about how everything had ended with my ex-boyfriend. I had only spoken to him once since leaving the U.S, and it was a very short and cold conversation. I found myself consumed with anger about the entire thing. Before coming to Australia, I had started reading Nelson Mandela's autobiography "A Long Walk to Freedom," and was thoroughly captivated and inspired by it. On most days I would lose myself in the pages of his book, reading more about his life and struggle. I noticed that the more I read the calmer and less angry I became. His story causes one to focus on the person in the mirror and take responsibility for one's own actions. I thought of all he had to endure, and how he used it to be a better person and not a bitter one. This inspired me to make changes in my life and alter my approach to life's disappointments, pain and suffering.

Many of us have an external force or figure in our lives that has the ability to transform and impact us in a positive way. We may never meet that person or force but the effect they can have is very real. Nelson Mandela is that force for me. I feel connected with his spirit and vision. The first time I heard of Nelson Mandela was through a small black and white television in Saint Lucia when I was ten years old. It was 1990, and he was walking side by side with his ex-wife Winnie Mandela with a raised fist above his head while thousands of people screamed and chanted out his name. I didn't fully understand then the true significance of his existence, but in 1998 he visited Saint Lucia, my very own homeland, for the first time, and although I was attending school in Barbados, I remember reading his speech in the local newspaper, and every word resonated with me. In his speech, one part stood out that inspired me to keep dreaming and believing in myself. He said that no matter who you are, or where you are from, you should not limit your dreams and aspirations to this small space. There is an entire world out there that is waiting for you to conquer it. I believe that quote rekindled my childhood dreams to one day travel and see the world.

When I was reading his book, I felt transformed. I exuded a sense of peace and calm that I did not even know lived within me. From that day, I let go of all the anger, not only towards my ex-boyfriend, but to anyone who I felt had caused me pain. I decided that I would be a victim of nothing, and a survivor of everything! I understood that I am the sum of all my experiences, and that everything is a part of God's master plan. It was a great release for me, and I was happy that I had found that peace, because a few years later I learned what betrayal felt like when my best friend moved on with that same ex-boyfriend.

It was one of the most painful things that I had ever experienced. Nothing hurts more than the feeling of betrayal by someone you love, and who you think loves you. I valued my friendship with her and was totally blindsided by her decision. Perhaps my purpose in their lives was for them to meet and find true love with each other---c'est la vie. I just wished that she had handled telling me differently, rather than through an unapologetic email. We were best friends, and she had been dating him for weeks and never mentioned it until I confronted her about it.

After she confirmed via email that she was indeed dating my ex-boyfriend, I cried all night. The next morning, I decided that I could either be consumed with anger which would only lead to destruction and my own demise, or I could turn my pain into power and move on with my life. I chose the latter. I never responded to her email, and I've never seen or heard from either of them since. It has been years since I've reflected on the issue, and it is something that I've moved on from, but it remains one of the most valuable lessons of my life. I can empathize with anyone who has had a broken heart.

10

The Places You Will Go If You Are Willing To Grow.

My circle of friends in Australia was diverse. It included my Aussie roommate Leah, a shy, Chinese girl name Tina, a young man from Malaysia named Kesh, and a feisty young woman from Nigeria named Mary. They all made my experience in Australia a lot more meaningful and allowed me to learn more about myself through their own uniqueness. I met new people every day, and it seemed like there was a student from every country in the world. Who knew Australia was such a popular place! Still, with all the people around me, I found myself feeling lonely. I had been single for a few months, so I spent a lot of time by myself. I decided to take up a new hobby. I created a blog and started writing about my experiences in Australia and my personal evolution. I shared pictures, journals and spoke candidly about things that I was interested in or passionate about. I connected with hundreds of people, and through that medium I realized my passion for writing and my ability to connect with others. I was at my happiest sharing my journey and experiences with the world. It seemed to inspire many and I slowly started to feel a greater sense of purpose that I had never felt before. People started writing to tell me how a particular journal entry had inspired or empowered them. It felt great that I was able to be a source of inspiration to others by just being myself. Slowly, it seemed, I was finding my place in the world and listening to my own voice.

We were approaching summer in Australia, and many were preparing for their summer vacations or internships and volunteer work. Earlier in the semester, my friend Mary from Nigeria told me about her experience as a young girl living and attending school in China. I thought this was fascinating. A young girl from Nigeria who lived in China and also spoke mandarin! There are some places that it´s difficult to imagine a certain race of people, and I just never imagined that black people lived in China. Some of her stories were quite funny, and it immediately triggered my interest. I began bombarding her with questions and wanted to know if it was possible for me to go there. She was very optimistic, and together we began working towards my summer trip to China. Mary had an uncle who lived and worked in China, so she contacted him to see if he could help in finding me a teaching position for the summer. He was very helpful and within weeks had found me a job as an English teacher at a University in a small town called Heshan, outside Guangzhou.

    I was really excited about this opportunity. I had heard about China as a little girl, but it seemed like another planet. I never imagined that I would one day get to visit. Although I was excited for the opportunity, I was concerned about how expensive such a trip would be. I decided to take a great leap of faith and use my housing allowance money for my schooling to finance my trip. I knew that I would have a job while in China, so my plan was to replace it then. I was taking a huge risk, but I thought it was one worth taking. Nothing great can be achieved without taking great risks. While preparing for my trip, I found out that I needed to have a visa. I was very concerned that I wouldn't receive it since I had a Saint Lucian passport. The requirements were quite stringent. Thankfully, I applied and within two weeks I received my visa. In July of 2005 I left Australia for my Chinese adventure. Since my friend Mary and Tina had given me a lot of information in advance, I felt comfortable that I would adjust accordingly. I knew that I needed to have an open mind, and I was in for a culture shock based upon some of their stories. When I arrived in China, I noticed from the immigration line that I would have to get used to the stares and pointing. People were staring, pointing, and even chuckling. Mainly Chinese of course, but it was mostly out of curiosity and excitement.

    Although there are a few black people living in China, it's still a novelty that most Chinese are fascinated with. I received the passport interrogation as in Australia, and it was there that the immigration officer asked me if Saint Lucia was a country! He was tough, and had a lot of questions. Later, Louis, Mary's Uncle and my new host, informed me that there were many people, especially Africans, who were migrating to China with fake passports, so they were extremely cautious. Before I entered the airport lounge, I stopped to use the ladies' room. My very first culture shock was staring me in the face! There was no toilet! It was a hole in the ground, and I would have to stoop! As a little girl growing up in Saint Lucia, I once had to use a similar bathroom, so it was not new to me, but it had been years, and I wouldn´t have imagined it being a way of life in China! Luckily, there was one toilet for foreigners, so I stood on the long line and waited my turn. One thing I realized from the beginning was that the Chinese were not very accommodating to foreigners. One would have to learn to adapt to their culture and way of life or get out. After all, it is a communist country!

11

There Is So Much Beauty In Not Knowing.

When I stepped out of the airport, my first reaction was, "Oh My God!" I had never seen so many cars and people in my life! And they all looked the same! They all seemed to be the same height, weight, and build. They even had the same expressions! The guys were pretty enough to be girls. They reminded me of the dolls I played with as a little girl growing up. Finally, the culture shock that I was waiting for! Many looked equally surprised to see me. I wondered what was going through their minds. My host Louis greeted me at the airport with some of his Chinese friends. Louis was a thirty-something year old man from Nigeria. He was like everything his niece Mary described him as, very much a gentle man and somewhat reserved. He was kind and gracious and from the beginning he did everything to make me feel comfortable. I felt very relaxed and at ease with him. Driving home, I felt like I had just been dropped in the middle of a human zoo. I was convinced that I would not make it home alive. Cars were driving in all directions, and there seem to be no sense of order and organization. It was complete chaos! Yet, everyone seemed to function quite well within that chaos. Louis and his friends looked completely relaxed in the car, while I buried my face in my hands. They found my reaction to the traffic amusing. I knew that this would definitely be a trip to remember.

When we arrived at Louis's apartment, I was surprised at how small everything was. Yet, his apartment was considered to be fairly large by Chinese standards. Louis was an engineer for a European company in China, and rented an apartment in Guangzhou where he lived on the weekends. On weekdays, he worked and lived on the company's compound about ninety minutes away in a town called Heshan. He offered to let me live in his apartment during my stay in China, for which I was extremely grateful. I couldn't have asked for a better guide in China than Louis. He attained his Master's degree in China, and had been living there for about five years, so he spoke the language fluently and had a great understanding of the people and culture. He was also a very calm, optimistic and caring person. From day one he took me under his wing and made me feel completely safe and at home. This allowed me to approach this unique cultural experience with optimism and an open mind. Guangzhou is a big and bustling city, and every day there was something new to discover. One of the things I liked about Guangzhou was that it was always alive. I can't recall a single day when I would go outside and there wasn't something going on, no matter what time it was. This gave me a better understanding of Chinese-Americans. They seemed to have a work ethic like no other. On any given holiday in the U.S, you can always count on the Chinese store and restaurant to be open. Chinese people do not seem to sleep! I guess the secret to long life is lack of sleep and hard work.

One of my most memorable experiences in China was at a train station. I was standing awaiting my train with Louis when an elderly man walked up to me, took my hands and began rubbing his fingers against it very hard. He did it repeatedly, and stared at his fingers to see if there was something there. I stood in amazement and started laughing. He was so old and fragile that I knew he was harmless, but I couldn't understand what he was doing. Louis, who had stepped away for a minute walked over and began laughing. He told me that some of the older folks have never seen a black person before, and sometimes they think that one's skin is covered in dirt, so they are simply curious. It had happened to him many times before. I found that to be funny, yet really sad. I couldn't imagine living in a world thinking only people like me existed, and then suddenly someone different appears. It almost sounds like what an experience with Aliens would be like. Who knows, perhaps that's what some of them thought we were. I later learned that because China is a communist country, most Chinese don't get to see anything but people like themselves on television, so some of them have never even seen a black person in their lives. I would later get a few similar reactions in the small town of Heshan where I taught. They were fascinated with me, yet very receptive. After about one week of sightseeing and getting to know more about the culture, I traveled to Heshan with Louis to meet the headmaster of the school where I would be teaching. On the way, Louis explained to me some of the disciplines in Chinese school and what would be expected of me. Of course, it is a Communist country so I had to stick with the guidelines i had been given and be careful of what I said. On our very first meeting, I was taken to lunch by the headmaster and some of the teachers and they explained what my job would entail. They were very friendly and gracious, and treated me like I was a celebrity of some kind. I was amazed by their reaction. They were very humble and did everything to make me feel welcome. I was told I would be teaching English to a class of about forty students. It seemed quite large, but for China it was relatively small. I was informed that my students were very excited to meet me and were all looking forward to my class.

On my first day of class, I got a huge welcome by all my students. They were all dressed up so nicely and neatly and when they saw me they cheered. Some of them even cried. I was completely overwhelmed and I couldn´t understand their reaction. I was just a simple girl from a small island who came to teach English, but to them, i was so much more. Most of them had never even seen a black person or a black woman. At the time my hair was braided, and they found it fascinating. They all wanted to have their hair braided too. Everyone gathered around and waited for me to speak. It was a lot more than the thirty students that I was anticipating, but I felt really comfortable right from the start. They all stared at me in total awe, and couldn´t stop smiling. In that moment, I had never felt more appreciated and useful.

I was so humbled by the experience to share their world. The funniest thing about being in front of the class was that they couldn't understand me and I couldn't understand them. They all had very little knowledge of English, but I learned quickly that the Chinese are an extremely determined people. They give everything their all and always go that extra mile. Most of them had already completed the entire activity book for the course period. By the end of the first class, they were introducing themselves and showing off some of their new vocabulary.

One of the funniest memories of my first day was selecting English names with my students. Many of them could not differentiate between common nouns and proper names, and would give themselves such names as Umbrella, Moon, Sun, Rain, and Sunset. One student insisted on being called Sarah, because he liked that name. As the saying goes, when in Rome, do as the Romans do. I went home that night feeling such a great sense of purpose and happiness. This was my general feeling for the entire time I taught there. Every day, someone did something that made me cry with joy. They were all so polite and gracious, and just wanted to learn English and more about the world. The most rewarding feeling for a teacher is having students who are excited and eager to learn. They had quite a few questions about the USA. Many of them thought that it was a bad and scary place, but it was still their dream to visit. They asked me if I was friends with any of the celebrities and what they were like. In their minds, just being from the USA made me a celebrity of some kind. Their innocence and naivety was pure and sacred, a part of me felt like there was beauty in that; the beauty of not knowing, like the first few innocent years of childhood.

It reminded me of when I first moved to the U.S. I came from my island somewhat shielded from many things. Even though I was forced to grow up quickly as a child, my island life shielded me from a lot of the prejudices and hatreds in the world. My first window of my innocence was through the eyes of a young girl I met my freshman year of college named Tiffany Cooper. She was from the Bahamas, but had lived in the U.S for many years. Although we were the same age, she seemed to have a vast knowledge and understanding of the world and things around her. I was in total awe of her independence and awareness of things I knew nothing of. Concepts like racism, anorexia, diets, and other everyday things were quite new to me. I knew that there were people of different colors and cultures, but I wasn't aware of how some people regarded people of color. I also couldn't understand how people suffered from a disease where they wouldn't eat, and I did not know what the word "calories" meant. I believe that by not knowing, I was protected from the impurities of the world, and it saved me from some of the pressures that I saw my friends struggle with. When I became aware, everything changed.

12

A Different Kind Of Love.

On most days, I looked forward to sharing my daily activities with Louis. He was a very easy person to speak with, and he loved my enthusiasm about teaching and being in China. He enjoyed listening to my stories and thought my passion for life was infectious. Slowly however, I realized that I started developing feelings for him that were more than just friendship. My perception of how I viewed men and relationships also started to change. Although I had only been in two serious relationships, I think the focus then was a lot more on external attributes rather than the internal. While they were both great guys, I believe I was initially attracted to their looks, achievements, style, and background more than anything else. The prerequisites society has set up for us when pursuing a relationship. All of these things are important in a relationship, but it often takes precedence over other things, like a person's character and goodness. For the first time, I believe I started to look past the external and started appreciating and loving the true quality of a man--- his character and inner beauty.

One of the things I loved the most about traveling around China with Louis was that he was well informed and knowledgeable about the people and culture. He gave me great insights about how the society functioned, and also how it was for expatriates living there. He was a smart man, and like no one I had ever met. He was well respected by his friends and colleagues, and had great leadership abilities. People found a sense of peace and comfort in his presence. I observed him and his actions and was impressed with his integrity and the way he treated others. Through his subtle example, I was able to improve areas within my own character which needed improving. I could see myself evolving into someone I wanted to be. He was making me better just by being himself. There is something uniquely beautiful about a man who is comfortable in his own skin and has a great sense of who he is. He was organized, disciplined, practical, yet open-minded. I would often tease him about being my financial advisor, as he always found ways to make my small earnings from teaching go further than I thought it could. With time, I found myself getting more attracted to him as a person. I loved more than anything that he was a man of his word. He talked the talk and walked the walk. My grandfather once mentioned to me when I was a teenager that all a man really has is his word, and if he cannot keep it and live up to it, then he shouldn't be taken seriously. These words of wisdom have been very useful in distinguishing true men of character and honor, versus men who say things that are simply pleasing to the ear to get their way. Although he was not my type physically, I found myself seeing past the physical and started to understand what is meant by inner beauty.

Louis was quite shy and reserved, so I was unaware for a while that he had developed strong feelings for me as well, although I was a bit suspicious. He never attempted to pursue me in any way, and was always the perfect gentleman. Growing up without the presence of a father in my life, I always appreciated men like Louis who made me feel safe and comfortable. As a child I adored my father. Although he and my mom were not in a relationship, I saw him often. In primary school, he drove me to school every morning, and for every birthday until the age of ten he would bring me a birthday cake and ice-cream at school to celebrate with my classmates. Such gestures meant the world to me and it's a memory I often reflect on when I think of him. However, he was not always a responsible father, but my mother never spoke of him in a negative way and always did everything to ensure that we maintained a relationship with him, even when he showed little effort or did not deserve it. Growing up, there were many things I overlooked about my father in the name of love, and to deny the sense of abandonment and feeling of being unloved, but as a teenager I was forced to face the harsh reality that the decision for him not being in our lives was one that he chose. Although his absence in my life did not prevent me from having a balanced and happy life, I know that it has had lingering effects and probably will affect me for the rest of my life. It is something that I have learned to accept and have made peace with. I love my father. He is a good man, but I wished that he had made better decisions. However, I harbor no anger or resentment towards him, and hope to have a stronger relationship with him one day. His decision to not be involved in the lives of his children is one that he and his conscience will have to deal with for the rest of his life. He lost so much more than we ever did. Every child needs and deserves a good father in their lives.

13

You Are A Name Brand All On Your Own---Accessorize Your Soul, Not Only Yourself!

A few weeks into teaching, I told my class that I was going to visit one of my dream attractions: "The Great Wall of China in Beijing!" They all jumped with joy and excitement, some even cried. I was startled by their reaction. I thought perhaps most of them had already been there or seen it, but to my surprise, none of them had visited, some of them had never even left their hometown of Heshan. Beijing was surprisingly a dream destination for most of them. Since China is a big country, getting from one state to the next is very expensive, which made it quite difficult for most Chinese who simply can't afford it with their small salaries. It made me realize how fortunate I was to be able to visit such a historical place, and I was determined to take full advantage of the opportunity. I promised that I would take many pictures so I could share the journey with them.

When I arrived in Beijing, I was greeted by pollution and noise. If I thought Guangzhou was a busy city, I was now in for a surprise. It seemed like all of China lived in Beijing. I was completely overwhelmed. Getting from the airport to our hotel was one of the longest and craziest car rides of my life. The hustle and bustle of Chinese life shows in every facet of their society. People are always on the go. It was a great relief when we arrived at our hotel. At this point, I was over the culture shock, and was simply trying to survive the chaos. Louis was in Beijing for a business meeting, and since visiting the Great Wall was one of the sites I had to see in China, I tagged along with him on his trip. I was very happy with my decision, because it would have posed quite a challenge for me alone. Louis spent a lot of time in business meetings, so I spent most of my time exploring the city on my own. The shopping was incredible. After all, everything is made in China right? There were an incredible variety of goods, and I was amazed at how inexpensive things cost compared to in the U.S. It is a shopping heaven for any girl who loves to shop. As much as I enjoyed it, it was sad having to experience it all alone. Sometimes I needed just to sit down and take everything all in. I wish I could have shared this with my family and friends. I know their reactions would have been similar to mine. I knew it would broaden their horizons and understanding of the world in a unique way. I wished more than anything that they were there with me.

One day while shopping in Beijing, I encountered someone on the street who wouldn't leave me alone. Usually, Louis would stand back and allow me to do my own shopping and sometimes negotiate with vendors for me, but this man was being rude and a bit aggressive. Louis exchanged a few words with him in Chinese, and the man walked away. I liked the way he handled the entire situation. He took charge and was firm yet gentle, and was able to command respect without being violent or aggressive. I was very impressed with that, and my feelings for him intensified even more. At dinner that night, I decided to ask him more personal questions about himself and his life. He was reluctant at first, as he is a private person by nature, but then he opened up. He was also quite funny and a lot more liberal than I had thought. His conservative personality caused me to think otherwise. The following day we explored the Great Wall of China.

When I first approached Tiananmen Square, I was overcome with awe, and I felt all the history and depth of that special place come over me. What a feeling! Upon approaching the Great Wall, people started walking up to me asking to take a picture with them. I was used to the attention by now, and was enjoying my new found fame. Before I knew it, there was a long line of people wanting to take a picture with me. Some American tourists walked up to me and asked, "Excuse me, are you a celebrity?" I smiled, and responded, "no, but I sure feel like one." At the time I wore my hair big and curly, and I think everything about me was new and unique to many of the Chinese, so it ignited their curiosity.

My first glance at the Great Wall took my breath away. I had seen it on television many times before, but in person it just seemed like a never ending stair way to heaven. I was completely blown away and took a moment to take it all in. There were thousands of people there on that day from all over the world. It felt like everything heaven would be like. There was so much laughter and joy in the air that in that moment, it felt like the only place on earth. I will never forget it. Louis and I climbed the wall as much as we could, until we were too tired to continue. With each step, I couldn't help but feel like I was living out my dreams. It was such a surreal feeling. *How did this all happen to a girl like me?* When we returned to Guangzhou Louis and I both knew of our feelings for one another, and our relationship took off from there. I was single for about one year, and had found happiness again. It was a great feeling, because I felt like I had evolved into another part of me. It was a part of me that needed to emerge, a deeper more meaningful side. When I returned with all the news and pictures of the Great Wall for my students, their joy filled me up inside. They could not contain their excitement, and as always they had a million questions. If they never saw me as a celebrity back then, they did now! They were in total awe of all the pictures and my enthusiasm over seeing the place. I think my experience made them believe that their dream of seeing the Great Wall was possible.

One day, after one of my classes, one of my students invited me to visit the factory where she worked. At that factory, they made clothing for major labels from all over the world. I was surprised to see how many leading clothing brands were being made in a factory in China, and by such young people. Everything was made in mass quantities and shipped out. It was another moment that put a lot into perspective for me. Some of us spend more than we can afford to keep up with the trends and a certain lifestyle and neglect to consider where and how these things are made, or if it is worth the astronomical prices that we sometimes pay. We condemn countries like China for human rights abuse, yet we spend millions of dollars outsourcing jobs there for small wages. These companies then brand, market, and sell their products at outrageous prices. Many of us, including myself back then, become victims of this brainwash marketing where we feel like we are defined by a brand or label, and get caught up in the hype.

Labels and brands become our lifestyle, and we often try to create a certain façade that showcases our superficiality while drowning us further in dept. After my visit to that factory, and witnessing what I had seen with my own two eyes, I couldn't go back to living that lifestyle ever again. It caused me to look at the bigger picture in life and ask myself some more tough questions. Who am I? Am I defined by who or what I wear? Do these things define me or make me? Am I less of a person without them? Am I less beautiful without them? How much is this lifestyle really costing me? When I began to answer those questions and stay true to myself, I made the necessary changes in my life.

Today, although I still love dressing up and looking great, I know that feeling great is even more important. Hence, I embrace a healthy and active way of life. I do more sensible shopping and I've become a strong advocate for "no name labels." I am my own brand! It's unique, beautiful, classy and created by me! I came to the conclusion that while it's ok to have favorite designers and brands; we shouldn't allow it to define who we are. We need to have an identity beyond all the branding, because when it's all taken off, we are just naked people in the mirror who are worth a whole lot more than clothes, shoes, and all the colorful accessories. Why not learn to first accessorize our soul before anything else?

14

Love Is Not Always Meant To Go The Distance.

I was on my final days in China. It was bitter sweet for me as I had gotten used to my new home and my new life, and since I had found a special someone to share it with, it was very difficult to leave. On the last day of school, my students had a farewell party for me with different activities. They showered me with many gifts and showed off their improved English skills. I was not sure how I would be able to find space in my suitcase for all their gifts, but I was so moved by their kindness and generosity that I knew I had to. Even with their small earnings, they went above and beyond to give me presents. These small acts really spoke of their nature. I had never felt more useful and appreciated in my life. This experience had changed me all for the better. I knew that for as long as I live, a small town named Heshan in China and its lovely people will always have a place in my heart.

I returned to Australia completely jet-lagged, but just in time for school. Louis and I had decided to give a long distance relationship a try, even though we were both apprehensive about it. After my experience in China, I felt a lot more comfortable in my program and had gained a broader perspective on things. I continued writing in the blog I had begun prior. Many wrote telling me about how my writing and how inspiring it was to them, and I started to realize that there were many people, including family and friends who started living vicariously through me. Hence, I was excited about seeing more of the world so I could share my experiences with them. I was not sure how I would be able to achieve that financially, but I had faith that the journey had only just begun. There was a lot more to discover and learn, and I wanted to experience it for myself.
A few months later, I traveled to Singapore to reunite with Louis. I had never seen such a clean place in my life. It was so clean and organized that you feel like you´re almost scared of dropping something. It was great to see him after a few months, but after corresponding via phone and internet for the past months, we had discovered a lot more differences than similarities in each other.

Although we both loved and cared for one another, our cultural differences and the long distance became an issue. Louis was from Nigeria, and even though he was educated, well-traveled and open minded, he still had his cultural value system instilled in him and had certain expectations of his partner and wife, which conflicted with my independent nature and my cultural practices. Although he had some of the great qualities that I wanted in a husband and one day the father of my children, I did not think it was enough to sustain us long term. It was a difficult decision for both of us, but when I returned from Singapore we decided to end our relationship. Nonetheless, he had added so much to my life that we remained friends. I distracted myself by keeping focused on school and building meaningful relationships with friends. Every day I was discovering new things about myself and others. I grew a lot closer to my friend Mary who complimented me in many ways. She was a strong personality and impressed me with her ability to balance her life in unfamiliar territories while staying true to herself. I also got quite close to a young man name Kesh from Malaysia who was a social butterfly, with a great sense of humor. We took wonderful road trips together, where he would tell me interesting stories about his strict grandmother who was Chinese, and the cultural differences with his mother's family who were Chinese and his father's family who were Indian. Most of his stories sounded similar to experiences from my own culture and people. His stories made me realize that we are more alike than we are different, and we all laugh and cry at the very same things. Another friend, Radhika, would often share stories of her life in India. Again I found similarities in their cultural practices with my own. Even their way of eating certain foods with their fingers, and the type of foods and music they listened to. India sounded like a fascinating place, and we both joked about visiting each other's homeland one day. Over the years we remained friends, and India still remains one of my favorite places in the world. I was on the final leg of my Master's program, and was busy working on my thesis. Toward the end of my program, I had almost run out of money, so I was living on a really tight budget.

My trip to China was not planned when I made my initial budget, so I knew that I would have to make major sacrifices for my remaining stay in Australia. I did not go out as often, and most of my friends rarely saw me. I did not want them to feel like they had to help out or pay my way through anything. I was taught by my mother that when you don't have things, you should learn to live without them. It's something I apply in my everyday life. Although we all need help sometimes, I don't think it's the responsibility of others to bail someone out of debt for things that are considered a luxury. I believe that unless it's an emergency of some kind, we should always try to live within our means and be happy with what we have. I knew my mom and family would be there for me if I asked, but I wanted to be responsible.

For about three months while working on my thesis, my diet consisted of crackers, bread, cereal, cheese and chocolate milk. My daily activities included my usual morning walks, and that was about it. It was a great relief when I completed my thesis. I was looking forward to going home. Graduation day was bittersweet. When I reflected on how far I had come, and my entire experience in Australia, I felt accomplished. It was a great feeling being in the company of my peers whom I had been intimidated by at first. I was proud that I completed the program and did not give up. I would encourage any young man or woman who would like to broaden their horizons to challenge themselves by exploring unknown and unfamiliar territories. There are great schools outside of North America and Europe, and the experience is priceless. The world is now a global village, and the opportunities are endless for anyone who is willing to challenge themselves and take great risks. Graduation day was a happy moment, but with a tinge of sadness because my friend Kesh was the only one who accompanied me to the ceremony. At the time, circumstances made it difficult for my mom and family to be there. I knew they were happy and proud of me, but I missed them and wish they could have shared that moment with me. It was their moment too.

15

We Can Have Plans, But Be Prepared For God´s Plans Too.

When the time came to leave Australia, I was ready to return home. It was a wonderful life-changing experience, but I was anxious to get back home and continue on my journey. My plan was to return to the U.S and apply for teaching jobs in China, where I intended to work for a year or two before pursuing a career as a Foreign Service Officer with the U.S Government. On my way home to the US, I stopped for a few days on the island of Fiji, since it was relatively close to Australia and on the way to the U.S. When I arrived at the airport, I thought Saint Lucia had been moved to the South Pacific! Everything about Fiji reminded me of my homeland. The people, the culture, the food, their customs, even their mannerisms were similar. I felt right at home and it was just what I needed as I had missed Saint Lucia dearly.

On the first night of my stay, I visited a local bar called "Ed´s bar." It was a popular night spot where all the tourists and locals went for live music and dancing. I ordered a drink and sat observing my surroundings while enjoying the reggae music. It was an outdoor bar with an indoor area for dancing. It felt a lot like home. I was in island heaven! I sat outside for a long time, and as I was about to leave for my hotel, I noticed that there was another room where people were drinking and dancing. I entered and stood in a dark corner observing everyone. From the corner of my eye, I noticed a short, white male approaching me. My first thought was, "I sure hope this short guy is not coming to bother me!" But he sure was, and insisted on buying me a drink. I refused the first time, but he came back having bought me one anyway. He tried talking to me over the loud music, which was a bit difficult, so we went outdoors to finish our conversation. His name was Michael and he was from Poland.

He immediately began chatting away. I found him to be quite funny and curious. A few minutes into our conversation, he leaned over and said, "listen, everyone is walking around this world wearing a mask, you and I are all the way on the other side of the world, and we are meeting for the first time and will probably never meet again, please let our conversation be the most honest one we've ever had." I found this statement to be powerful. It was just what I needed to hear, as I was at a place in my life where I felt like everyone was walking around with a mask on. People seemed so afraid to reveal their true selves.

After my relationship with Louis had ended, I definitely was not interested in meeting anyone, let alone in starting a relationship. My mind was focused on my career and seeing more of the world. But as always, life happens when we least expect or are not looking. After Michael made that statement, I smiled and agreed, and I felt an instant attraction to him. I am impressed by a beautiful mind more than anything else. We both started talking about life, our journey and what brought us to Fiji.

It was very easy to speak with my new found friend. He was open, direct and seemed honest. He spoke candidly about his past mistakes, and seemed like he had come around in full circle. I shared my journey thus far with him and spoke of my own struggles with life. It was refreshing meeting someone like him who was open-minded, curious and honest. With every passing minute, he became more and more attractive to me. He had a cute face with the most beautiful blue eyes that I had ever seen, but I couldn't help keep thinking in my mind, "why does he have to be so short?" I then remembered the wonderful experience that I had with Louis, and how worthwhile it was seeing beyond the external and appreciating the true beauty of someone which comes from within, so I quickly dismissed all those thoughts, and embraced the moment and continued to learn more about him.

We talked for about two hours or more, and when we proceeded to take a cab home, we found out that we were staying at the same hotel. We shared a cab, and stayed in the hotel lounge area and talked until the sun came up. It was one of the most thought provoking and meaningful conversations that I've ever had with someone. We talked about everything; relationships, culture, people, traveling, success, failure, winning, losing, and everything of substance. We both loved to talk, so time flew by like the wind. He was funny without even trying, and I couldn't stop laughing at his slightest gestures. I noticed that he was a bit hyper-active, and his reaction to the simplest things was like a kid's reaction to a new toy.

There was something so pure and magical about that to me. Everything about him was unique and different and I was intrigued. It felt great having such an in depth conversation with a complete stranger. At the end of our conversation, I wondered if I would ever see him again, but I knew that I would never forget him. I wasn't sure where this curious, hyper, funny guy from Poland had emerged from, but he made a lasting first impression on me, and had slowly planted footprints in my heart.

With my son Matthew and friends in Marakesh Morocco.

At the Great Wall of China.

Sitting in front of the Taj Mahal In India.

With my students in Japan.

Kourion Amphitheater, Cyprus.

Kissing my beautiful mom in front of the Trevi Fountain in Rome Italy.

Visiting the Pyramids in Cairo Egypt.

With Japanese students in Kimono wear.

Outside Nelson Mandela's prison cell on Robben Island in Cape Town South Africa.

Michael, Matthew and I in Mauritius. Photo used for CNN Article.

16

An Encounter with an Angel.

The following day, I learned that Michael had booked a few days on one of Fiji's many private islands, and I had done the same, but unfortunately, they were different islands, and by the time he was scheduled to return, I would have already left for the U.S. We said our goodbye's in the hotel lobby that morning and exchanged email addresses. I placed his email address in a small bible I took with me everywhere I went, and left Fiji for the U.S. On my way back home, I stopped in California for a few days to visit a friend. I spent a long time talking about Michael with her. When I arrived in L.A, I knew that he was still in Fiji and wouldn't have internet access for a few days, but he did mention that once he got back to New Zealand he would email me. I decided to email him anyway to say hello. A few days later he responded, and he was just as excited to hear from me as I was to hear from him. Over time, our conversations became a daily ritual, and things were moving along quite quickly. Michael was in his thirties and had a good idea of what he needed and wanted, and he was convinced that he had found it. I was in my twenties and not searching for love, but somehow it seemed to have found me. This was not aligned with my plans or the goals I had set out for myself, but I could slowly feel myself drifting away, and I was happy to do so.

When I returned to Florida, I settled in and began looking for a job. My mind was still focused on returning to China, but when I returned to the U.S from Australia, I was told that since I was a permanent resident, I was not permitted to live outside the U.S for more than one year, and in order to do, I would have to apply for my citizenship. This meant that I would have to commit to at least nine months in the U.S to receive my citizenship before leaving for China. I had given myself a minimum of three months to get everything prepared to return to China, but this news meant that I would have to re-prioritize. I immediately filled out the application for my U.S citizenship. In the meantime, I was busy applying for a job in my field. Michael and I kept talking on a regular basis, and things seemed to be moving along pretty quickly. He wanted me to visit him in Sweden as soon as time permitted. Although everything was moving along quicker than I anticipated, I could not deny this voice in my head telling me to give it a try. A few weeks later, I was on a flight to Sweden via Paris.

On the flight to Paris, I felt unusually ill. My head was spinning and I felt weak. When the plane landed, I still felt sick, but a bit relieved. I thought that the worst was behind me. However, while on the shuttle bus at the airport to board my connecting flight to Sweden, I started to vomit. I was so weak that I couldn't sustain myself, and fell to the floor. I kept throwing up all over myself and hand luggage. There were people standing around me trying to avoid coming into contact with my vomit, and three young ladies were even laughing while they huddled themselves in a corner to avoid me and my vomit. In that moment, a beautiful young woman walked up to me and started wiping my mouth and face with her handkerchief. Since I was so weak and a bit disoriented, I held on to her with my vomit stained body and clothes. She embraced me, and not once did she show any sign of disgust or frustration. I kept apologizing, and couldn't stop crying. My tears were not just from feeling sick, but from experiencing true compassion from this Good Samaritan.

My heart was filled with gratitude and I felt such intense love for what was a complete stranger. After she cleaned me up, she held on to me and my luggage and got me to the security checkpoint safely. I felt a little better and we spoke for a short time before she went on to board her flight to Italy. We exchanged emails and have kept in touch ever since. Today, Kate is a doctor and I am certain that anyone who is placed in her care will know what it's like to experience humanity at its best. Kate's act of compassion towards me changed my approach to others also. Such acts of kindness cannot be ignored or forgotten, and because of Kate, I am better than I was before. Angels live among us every day. They come to our rescue and even save our lives. Often, they are complete strangers, yet they can have the greatest impact. In everyday situations, and even when others are difficult and unkind, I try to remember Kate's act of kindness towards me through her own example and her beautiful nature. I've learned that sometimes when people behave in an uncivilized and destructive manner, all they simply need is a subtle example of what it means to be a good human being.

When I arrived in Sweden, I felt like my normal self again. It was wintertime and it was dark, cold, and rainy. There was nothing much to see but snow, but I was very excited about that as I had never seen snow before. As a child I always imagined what snow felt like. It seemed fascinating and I thought that if I ever got to see and feel it that I would eat a lot of it, because it looked like cotton candy. I will never forget my reaction when I held it in my hands for the first time. It still looked like cotton candy, but didn't feel or taste anything like it. It just felt and tasted like ice and water! A part of me was happy that it took me this long to see snow for the first time. I realized that some things look and feel better in our imagination than they do in person. I loved watching Michael's reaction to how I responded to things for the first time. It became a new goal for him to show me all the things that I had never seen.

My visit to Sweden was short, so we tried to do as much exploring as we could. Michael was fascinated by my comparisons of European, Caribbean, and American culture. In Europe, everything seemed extra small, and most people walked around with frowns on their faces, like every day was a funeral. I couldn't understand it. Michael said that the weather had a lot to do with, but I thought that it was because the people were simply miserable and unhappy. Although Michael and I had spent countless hours on the phone and on video chats, it felt good spending time with him in person, and it felt even better to confirm our connection and love. Every day I got to know more about him and grew more in love with him. He was different from any guy I had ever met.

It was my first time seriously dating someone outside my race, and I found it refreshing that he was comfortable with expressing his feelings and showing intense emotion, which was not something I was used to. He was very loving, attentive, and caring, and wanted to do everything within his power to make me happy. It was a welcome feeling. I loved the experience of being loved in such an open way. I was able to be myself in every way. My visit was coming to an end, and about one day before I left for the U.S, Michael gave me a promise ring, which he said was a covenant of our love. I returned to the U.S and started actively searching for a job, but I was feeling a little off balance, because my life had taken a different course than I had planned. Michael was also a bit demanding and the pressures of a serious relationship began to weigh heavily on me. I wanted to get a job in my field, but that would require me to accept a long term position, but I also had plans on returning to China in a few months, so I was thinking maybe a temporary job would be best. On top of everything there was Michael asking me every day when will we meet again. I found myself on a road with no signs. I could barely hear my own voice anymore. How was I going to balance this new life? After a few weeks, I got a job offer in Florida, but was told that I would have to sign a contract for two years.

    I spoke with Michael about it and he opposed me accepting the job as he wanted me to return to Sweden to spend the summer with him. I found myself at a fork in the road. I was excited about getting my first job after graduate school, but then I wanted to give this new found love with Michael a chance. I was curious as to what awaited on the horizon. I also thought that Michael was a lot more pushy and demanding than what I was used to, but I figured it was simply the uncertainty of our situation. I felt at crossroads with everything and it was difficult to make a decision. I had always been an independent person and never felt obligated to ask my partner about such decisions before, but I questioned if that was my downfall in my past serious relationships. I wondered if my need for total independence and not wanting to live my life within any parameters was being selfish. I always felt like I had to do what was in my best interest and conducive to my overall happiness and fulfillment. However, this time I was questioning and doubting myself. Maybe I was being too tough. Maybe I was taking the whole "strong independent woman" label to an extreme. Maybe I just needed to be more selfless and less in control.

    In the end, I declined the job offer and decided to spend the entire summer in Sweden instead to build more on our relationship. It was a decision I would question for many years. Deep inside, I was holding on to a little bit of resentment against Michael, but I said nothing. I felt like I was forced to choose, when I was not prepared to do so, but then I thought of Michael's words, "opportunities would always be there, but love probably won't."

17

A Whole New World.

I arrived in Sweden again in the summer and everything was in full bloom. It felt like a completely different country. Everything was bright and green. Sweden is a beautiful, clean country, covered with lakes and nature in abundance. There is something so serene, tranquil, and magical about it. Although very quiet, it has its own unique charm that I greatly enjoyed. My summer days were long, since Sweden experiences long days of sunlight in the summer. The sun rises about four in the morning and sets at about eleven at night. It was fascinating to me at first, but it has a down side; the long winter months of cold and darkness. My summer was filled with beautiful afternoons by the lakes, long walks and road trips. I was getting to know a lot more about Michael, and we were building on our love. We also planned to do a lot of traveling that summer. We both had a strong desire and passion to see the world and learn more about different cultures; after all, we did meet half way across the world, so this common goal and desire brought us even closer together. We first did a road trip through Europe, which was a bit ambitious for both of us. It was many hours of driving and there was a lot to do and see in the few weeks that we had. Nevertheless, it was one of the most memorable things that I've ever done in my life and one that will live with me always.

Europe is a fascinating continent. Every country has its own beauty and charm, and the diversity and multiculturalism makes it one of the most interesting places in the world. One moment we were driving on the autobahn in Germany, and the next through the plains and countryside of France, then through the mountain regions of Austria and Switzerland, and then the winding hills of Italy. Driving through the countryside was breathtaking. I couldn't help but think what a beautiful world we live in. I was so happy that I was able to see and experience it. It was just like everything I imagined as a child. When we returned from our long road trip through Western Europe, we decided to visit Egypt. Going to Egypt was a surreal experience for me. I had seen the great pyramids on television, heard about the Egyptians and pharaohs and even Cleopatra, but I never imagined that a girl like me would ever visit this place. It was one of those moments where I felt like I was really living out my dreams.

We arrived in Egypt and went through the routine interrogation with immigration. This time it was even more intense than before. There was a debate about whether I needed to have a visa to enter the country. After about an hour of questioning, I was finally allowed to enter. We explored the cities of Luxor, Hurgardur and Cairo. While each of these cities had their own distinct character, Cairo was the most mind blowing. Our eight hour bus ride from Hurgardur to Cairo was a bit scary as a police escort was needed. This was to prevent any terrorist attacks. It was in the middle of the night, and everything about it was uncomfortable and terrifying. When we arrived in Cairo, I was completely stunned by how much everything was ruined or destroyed. I had expected to see ancient monuments that were crumbling in places, but i was not prepared for the contemporary communities that were ruined by war, poverty and neglect. Between the heat, the millions of people and all the chaos surrounding me, I felt like I was on another planet. Some countries do feel like they are detached from the rest of the world, and that's how it felt in Egypt. When I first saw the pyramids up close I had to take a moment to take it all in. How did a girl like me get to see and experience this? I felt so fortunate and once again I wished that I could share this moment with family and friends.

Michael and I were both in total awe of it all and took some time to explore it; we even made the narrow climb inside the Keophs pyramid which was quite scary, but worth it. Egypt is country rooted in history and depth, and those memories are ones I will always treasure. When we returned to Sweden, we continued to enjoy our last days of summer and prepared for my departure. It had been a wonderful and exciting summer, but deep down, there was also a feeling of sadness. I was no longer feeling like I was in the driver's seat of my own life. Although I was getting to live out my dream, it all seemed to have been happening too quickly. While one of my dreams was to travel the world, I wanted to have a balanced life as well. I had recently graduated, and was looking forward to accomplishing all the goals I had set out for myself in terms of having a successful career and fulfilling my true purpose. Yet, my life seemed to have taken a different course. As a child, I was told the Cinderella story like almost every other little girl. And somewhere in our sub conscious most of us grow up dreaming and waiting for our own Prince Charming to sweep us off our feet and live happily ever after. I was no different, and sometimes it felt that way with Michael while traveling the world, but I was starting to realize that perhaps it came at a price that I was not sure I was willing to pay--- my freedom. That summer I gained fifteen pounds. I think I found comfort in food to hide some of the pain I was feeling inside. I was used to being challenged either by work or school, but it was a relaxed summer and i was not doing much, so i used food to fill the void.

Michael teased me about my weight gain, but he always made me feel comfortable and did not make it an issue. In fact, he thought it suited me a lot better. It was one of the reasons why I loved him. He always made me feel comfortable with myself no matter the circumstances. It had been one of the most adventurous summers of my life, but also an eye- opening one. It seemed God was giving me all my heart desires, but I was beginning to question if it was all what I really needed and wanted. Michael and my relationship was now a serious one, and we had gotten over the honeymoon phase and started dealing with the real issues and differences in a relationship: personality, age, culture, geography, religion, and the other usual struggles. Although there were some things that concerned me about him, they were not enough to outweigh his good qualities. I returned to the U.S not knowing what the future held for us, but we remained committed to each other in every way.

18

So Many Roads--- Not One Sign.

When I returned to the U.S, I decided to move to Chicago to seek employment. I had two friends who lived there, and we thought that I would have better opportunities in my field in Chicago than in Florida. I had never lived in any other state than Florida, so this was a new experience for me. Everything about the Midwest was different from Florida, and I was not sure if I would like it there very much, but I was willing to try. I have never been a fan of city life, and since my friends stayed in downtown Chicago, I knew that it would be a major adjustment, but I packed my bags and made the move. I shared an apartment with my college friends Paul and Moe, and it was a pleasure living with them as they both had a great passion for life. Moe is a Thai-American who is like a walking encyclopedia and seemed to be well versed on every topic. Paul is a Caucasian-American, who I often compare to Einstein because of his remarkable and unique mind. It was an absolute joy to be in the presence of those two eccentrics. They both added so much laughter and joy to my world, and we all got along great.

At the time, I was actively looking for work, but still feeling completely lost. Michael was pressuring me about moving to Sweden, and we spent countless days and nights arguing over how this could work for both of us. I wanted to maintain my independence, and Michael wanted to maintain his stability. I was very apprehensive at first, because the thought of moving to a foreign land without a job and a support system outside of my partner was a bit scary. Michael saw it as an excuse and me being selfish.

I suggested that he moved to the U.S, but at the time, he felt that since he had a more established life in Sweden, it would be better if I moved. That made sense, but while I was younger and had the flexibility to make such a move, it was still a big step having to give up a life that I was familiar with and start all over in an unknown land. While I am usually open to change, this one seemed like I would be giving up a big part of my own independence and identity to someone else. I was not sure I was prepared to do that. As time went by, my life seemed to be at a standstill. I was going to interviews, but had not received any job offers. I then shifted my focus from career jobs to temporary employment since after months of debating with Michael; I had finally agreed to move to Sweden.

Earlier in the year, I had applied for my U.S citizenship, and we agreed that once I had completed the process that I would then move to Sweden. In the meantime, I began to prepare for my new life mentally and spiritually. While in Chicago, I was determined to find a way to attend the Oprah Winfrey Show. She had always been a great role model for me, and I thought that since I lived right down the street, that it would be great if I got to see a live taping. I went online and applied to be in the audience, and luckily I was selected. I went to a live taping, where Bono, Alicia Keyes and Kanye West performed to promote Oprah's red campaign. It was an amazing experience getting to see a live taping. Oprah was her usual enthusiastic self and seemed quite down to earth. A few weeks later, my friend Paul received free tickets from a friend who worked at the show, and we accompanied him again as guests for the taping. The subject of the show was the book, *The Secret*.

The book had recently been released and was the latest publishing phenomenon. This show was different from the first. While I thought the book was quite inspiring and empowering, it took me back to my impression of most Americans when I first moved to the U.S. The constant feeling of emptiness and the need to be refilled and inspired. It was yet another self help guide to live a happy and fulfilled life. And with Oprah supporting such an initiative, it spread like wildfire, and suddenly it was no longer a secret. Everyone seemed to have found the answer to attracting all of their heart's desires by employing what the book referred to as the "power of positive thinking." The extraordinary success of the book spoke volumes about the power of marketing and branding, because this concept, in my opinion, was no secret and had been in existence for a long time. I left the live taping feeling disappointed. Since I was preparing for my move to Sweden, I had given up on searching for career jobs and decided to find a regular job to earn some money until my time came to leave. All these sudden changes had me feeling a bit off balance, but I embraced the changes.

One afternoon while discussing the preparations for my move to Sweden with Michael, he seemed less enthusiastic than before. He started to express his concern about certain things like me adjusting in Sweden with the weather, culture, finding employment, and other changes. All of these things did concern me at first, but Michael convinced me that it would be ok, and I slowly came around. Now, it seemed the realities of everything were becoming apparent to him and he was having cold feet. After that conversation, I started to question the wisdom of making such a life-changing move, given his "wishy-washy" behavior, so I decided to refocus on my original goals and get back on track. I started applying for jobs, this time abroad. Before I met Michael, my plan was to return to China to teach, so I thought that I would get back on course, and continue to pursue my dreams. While searching for jobs online, several opportunities for teaching in Japan started coming up. I was impressed by the structure of things in Japan, and the pay was a lot better than in China. I applied to a few jobs, and surprisingly, I started receiving calls the same day. One job in particular stood out for me.

It was to work as a primary school English teacher in the town of Gotemba . They provided a car and an apartment, which was quite impressive. I immediately applied and got a response the same day. After a few conference calls and a long application process, I was offered the position. I was now preparing for my new life in Japan instead of Sweden. Although I had been offered the position, and was preparing for my trip to Japan, I had not yet received my citizenship, so once again I was taking a leap of faith. I still had a few more weeks before I would have to leave, and somehow, I knew that I would receive it on time. While preparing for my departure, I got an opportunity to work for a few months in Atlanta. It was great for me to earn some extra money, so I packed my bags and moved to Atlanta for two months. Michael was not very happy with my decision to move to Japan, and for a while things were a bit tense. I felt that his uncertainty about my move to Sweden was not a solid foundation on which to plan a life-changing move. I was a bit disappointed in him as well, as once again I felt like I had to make plans to accommodate him on short notice because of his doubts.

While in Atlanta, I was called in for my citizenship interview, and I became a U.S citizen. It was a wonderful feeling to be a citizen of country that had given me so much. I felt in every way that I was also an American and supported the ideals that the country was founded on. And although I sometimes liked to question the status quo and I often challenged convention, I am grateful for the free speech that America guarantees me. There simply is no other country like it in the world. After my two months in Atlanta, I returned to Chicago to get ready for Japan. I had already said my goodbyes to my family in Florida, so the only thing left to do was leave. My best friend Cardine flew over to help me pack and see me off. Cardine and I are cousins and grew up in Saint Lucia together. We both moved to the U.S around the same time, and we've always maintained a very close friendship. When I sit and reflect on the most important times in my life, highs and lows, she was always right there next to me. With her, I've always felt like I could be myself in every sense of the word. I could always count on her and know that she will always be there for me in good and bad times. And while we are complete opposites, she adds so much to my world and she is one of the few people I can't imagine my life without. Everyone should have a friend like Cardine.

19

Not Everything Is For Everyone.

When I arrived in Japan, I was amazed by how clean and organized everything was. At the airport in China, there seemed to have been a lot more chaos compared to Japan. Thankfully, the entire immigration process went smoothly, and before I knew it I was outside awaiting my bus to my new hometown of Gotemba. While I stood and awaited my bus, I couldn't help but notice how well groomed everyone was. The women were neatly dressed and the men looked smart in their suits. Another thing that immediately drew my attention was how punctual the Japanese are. The bus arrived at the scheduled time, and not one minute later. It was an absolute pleasure sitting on the bus. It seemed brand new, and was so clean that one could eat off the floor.

On my drive from Tokyo to Gotemba, I enjoyed the scenic views and took in my unusual surroundings. It was like a whole new world. The people looked so different from me, yet they were doing the same things that people were doing all over the world on any given day. People were going to work, children were going to school, and the stores were busy with the usual hustle and bustle. Many Japanese express themselves boldly in the latest fashions, which were fascinating. While the young people had a liberal attitude with their style of dress, preferring eye-catching colors, patterns, and accessories, the older folks were clearly more conservative. It was early in the morning, and although I was tired from my flight, I was wide awake with curiosity. I was feeling good about my new home and couldn't wait to start exploring.

When I arrived in Gotemba, I was greeted by the school's secretary who picked me up at the train station. Gotemba was like a village compared to Tokyo, but it was great being away from the busy city life. The secretary Toyo, was pleasant and gracious, and used her limited English to inform me about what my next few days would be like in my new home. There was much to do, as I needed to get many things organized for my apartment and for work. My apartment was very small, but I loved the entire theme of it all. It was compact, simple and practical. I loved the design, which seemed authentically Japanese. They seemed to have made great use of all available space and although it was small, I didn't feel the need for anything else. I learned quickly the truth behind the adage that less is more. When Toyo left, I looked out my little window and saw this magnificent mountain with a snow-capped peak glowing in the distance. It was the famous Mt Fuji! I could hardly believe it! I was living at the foot of Mt Fuji! And I would get to wake up to it every single morning. It felt like something out of a storybook. I lay on my bed and could hear nothing but the sound of my heavy breathing. It was completely silent. Suddenly, I felt my building move. I thought maybe it was only in my mind, but then it moved again. It was an earthquake, and it was very scary. I later learned that it was something that I would have to get used to in Japan as it happened often.

    I didn't have internet or phone service for a few days, so I knew that the first few week would be a long one, and one of reflection. This was customary on my journey, and I liked taking the time to reflect on everything. On the small television, there were only three channels and everything was in Japanese, so it was just me and my thoughts. I took a walk around my community of tightly clustered houses, and I felt like a giant next to everyone and everything. In Japan everything seemed like it had been condensed to accommodate its people and their small stature. There were streams flowing throughout the town, and they provided a sense of calm and peace all around. Every time I entered a store, the shop keepers were always so gracious and humble. Most bowed their heads to greet and welcome me. I felt completely relaxed and at ease. I loved their civil nature and great humility.

    As the days went by, a few more of the new teachers arrived, and the atmosphere started to feel a little more relaxed. One of the teachers who lived in the apartment next to me was a guy named Daniel from Australia. He was an easy going, calm, funny young man who I instantly connected with. At first, we got along so well that I even thought he had a crush on me, and I was feeling flattered by the idea. A few days later, I had a rude awakening when he mentioned that he was gay. I had a good laugh at myself, because since I have a few gay friends, I always felt like my "gay-dar" was well-tuned, but this proved not to be the case. During my stay in Japan, Daniel became my closest friend and I learned so much from him. There were teachers from all over the world. Most I encountered were either from the U.S, Great Britain, Canada, or Australia. I believe that the Japanese experience is such a unique and life-changing one that the recruitment of teachers should be from a wide range of English speaking countries e.g. the Caribbean and Africa, so that everyone could experience it. Most recruiters seem to favor teachers from first world countries. I think it´s sad that had I not had an American passport that I would have been denied such a great opportunity even if I had the same qualifications.

One of the first things that I observed about Japan was that it is a place that one has to conform to, as the Japanese do not in any way adjust to foreigners. Some things proved to be difficult at first, like suggesting inventive or innovative approaches to something, or taking initiative when needed. The Japanese culture is a collective one where everyone has a systematic way of doing things, which is rarely questioned or changed. Coming from a country like the U.S where everything is questioned and where change is seen as inevitable, it was not easy to conform, and that was a great challenge for me. However, I think that anyone who gets to live within the Japanese culture learns the true art of adaptation and compromise. After a few days I was given my car and was shown the five different schools in which I would be teaching. I was responsible for grades one through eight. On most mornings, while driving through the small town of Gotemba in my typical small Japanese car, I would marvel at my surroundings with all its flowing streams, small carefully tended gardens, and peculiar buildings and feel a great sense of happiness. Although it was an entire differently world, I felt at home.

I loved teaching in Japan. The structure and organization of things was different from China, and the overall experience was a unique and interesting one. I especially liked the fact that I was responsible for creating and implementing my own lessons, which allowed me to be as creative with teaching as I wanted to be. One of the great things about teaching English in China and Japan is that everyone is so excited to learn English. Both the children and adults alike. They were all eager to learn and always looked forward to my class. This enthusiasm created a wonderful atmosphere for teaching, and made me feel needed, knowing that so many people were depending on me to enrich and broaden their knowledge.

As time went by, everything became familiar and it felt like I had been doing it for years. I loved teaching, and I connected very well with my students. I believe they were just as fascinated with me as I was with them. I loved how they would all chuckle and whisper to each other every time I walked into their classroom and stare at me with certain awe in their faces. I always wondered what went through their imaginative minds. As a child, I was fascinated with people who looked different from me. In fact, I thought they were all from another planet, so perhaps that's what they thought of me. I noticed a pattern while teaching. The younger the children, the more open, enthusiastic, bold, and expressive they were. The older they were, the harder it was to get them to open up in any way.

Japanese are naturally shy people, so convincing the older children to speak out was quite a task. Another thing I admired was how disciplined and respectful the students were. When a teacher walked into the classroom they all stood up and gave a warm greeting, and did the same when leaving. They followed the rules very well and were always prepared for learning. Sometimes, the uniformity of the culture became a little trying for me, as sometimes one hoped for there to be some room for change, but that's one of the areas where you are forced to adjust and adapt, as nothing should interfere with the Japanese order of things. At lunch time, all teachers were obligated to eat lunch with their class in a hall filled with students. Every day a new class was responsible for serving lunch to their peers. I got the same portion of food as my students and ate when they did, and left when they were finished.

At first, it was a new and different experience, seeing them with their heads covered in their hair nets walking around with their aprons on, but at times I yearned for a moment where I could have just sat and enjoyed my meal in peace. However, the great thing about stepping out of one's comfort zone and living in unfamiliar territories is learning to appreciate the things that we take for granted. I was slowly learning just how lucky we are in the U.S, and some of the things that we think are normal, are really a privilege.

While I adjusted to my environment, I missed the liberty and freedom to express myself as I desired. As unique and wonderful as the experience was, sometimes I felt like I was chained in and living a robotic life. One has to be born and raised in such a culture to fully understand and embrace it. I believe that it is easier for someone to move from a communist or socialist society into a democratic one, than for someone coming from a democratic society to adapt to a socialist and communist culture. These things require time, patience and a strong ability to conform.

Sometimes, the differences out-matched my ability to accept certain things and I found myself complaining a lot and finding it difficult to adjust. While I was making the best of the experience, I think I truly learned to have a greater appreciation for the freedoms I was blessed with in the U.S. Although sometimes I was frustrated with the excess and waste of American culture, I still had the choice to change or rebel against it if I chose to, but in countries like Japan you learn quickly that it's their way or the highway, and you are forced to adapt to the order of things even if it makes absolutely no sense. This was something I had the most trouble with. For example, pedestrians have to wait for a signal to cross the street. One day, while standing at a light with no traffic, I stood with about five other Japanese awaiting the signal to cross. For about five minutes we stood there waiting for the signal and it did not appear. Not a single car passed during that entire time.

It was obvious after seven or eight minutes that the signal was not functioning as it should. I decided to cross. They all looked at me with this scornful look on their faces in disapproval at my decision to cross before the signal appeared. I went into the store to purchase my goods, returned, and they were still obediently standing there! They refused to cross without the signal, even though they knew it was not working. I found the entire situation amusing. This example of conformity and extreme adherence to the rules was one of the things that infuriated me the most about Japan. One thing that I've learned living in a socialist culture is when you train people to behave and act like robots, in situations where common sense is needed, and even if they are the smartest people in the world, they will still act like robots.

Still, there was a certain charm and tranquility about Japan that I enjoyed and needed. Their peaceful nature and disciplined way of doing things ultimately becomes a part of you, and you slowly learn to appreciate the simpler and more meaningful things in life. Japanese people value life and it is shown in their lifestyle. You can always find the young and old alike outdoors exercising or meditating. They always try to keep active. Their diet is very healthy and their foods are a lot more fresh and natural. I looked forward to my long walks and overall felt the healthiest I had ever been. I had a certain peace and happiness in Japan that I did not feel in a very long time. Less is indeed more.

20

We Should Not Expect Change, If We Refuse To Change.

When I moved to Japan, Michael and I were estranged in our relationship. He was not happy with my decision, and was disappointed that I chose to move to Japan and not Sweden. The first few weeks were tough for us, as we spent most of our time on the phone arguing over the issue. Over time, however, we agreed that I would move to Sweden when my contract in Japan ended. It was a relief not having to argue about this issue any more, and having that constant pressure from him. I shared my everyday life stories in Japan with him as he was fascinated with Japanese culture. A few months later he visited me in Japan. It was a pleasant culture shock for him as he explored my new surroundings. One day, I decided to take him on a nature walk with me and my students. They were all fascinated with him. They couldn't stop touching his hair and looking into his blue eyes. Michael explored other major cities in Japan, and immersed himself in the culture. It was one of the things that kept us connected, our desire to see the world and learn more about other people and cultures. I admired his ability to find his way around the globe and see the beauty in things most people overlook. He has a special eye for beautiful things and would capture the most intriguing pictures on our journeys. He often used me as his muse for his photography, which I enjoyed since I love taking pictures, and thankfully I now have a memorable collection.

While Michael was in Japan, we talked more about my move to Sweden in the near future and building on our life together. We also talked more about marriage, since Michael had given me a promise ring a year before. Although there were quite a few odds against us, we were both committed to our relationship and trying to make it work.When Michael returned to Sweden, I started to question my decisions. He had this way of making me feel guilty about being hesitant to move to Sweden and starting a family. Being married and having a family was something I dreamed of and looked forward to more than anything, but I didn't want it to be dictated by society or anyone else. I wanted it to be when I felt ready in every single way. I was feeling a sense of guilt and pressure that was weighing heavily on my mind and heart. In Japan, I spent a lot of my time with my friend Daniel. I love surrounding myself with people whom I believe challenge me to be better, and Daniel had this calm, positive, and patient demeanor that made everyone feel at peace in his presence. He was also a good listener, and I would usually share my thoughts about life and all its wonders with him. Although we were from two different continents, we got along great. We often explored our surroundings together and would marvel at the peculiarity of Japanese culture. We took long road trips and sang loud in the car to our favorite music. One of the things we loved to do was eat out. We spent a good portion of our salaries trying various cuisines and filling our appetites.

One day I was expressing my frustration to Daniel at my mother's constant need to be a savior to others which made it hard to get the focus and attention from her that I needed. Daniel then expressed his frustration at his mother's over-eagerness to solve his problems for him, and how it sometimes frustrated him and made him feel a bit helpless. In that moment, I realized how difficult it is to be a parent, especially a perfect one. My mother probably was unaware that her constant need to help others was alienating me, and Daniel's mother probably thought that by always trying to help her son that she was being the best mother in the world. As parents, all we can do is to do the best we can, and somewhere along the road, children will learn to understand our shortcomings. We definitely cannot please everyone, no matter how much we love them.

In Japan, I spent a lot of time reflecting on my life and the changes that I needed to make within me. I also spent a lot of time writing about it in my blog. I could feel myself developing into an even deeper side of me. I started concentrating on the areas that I felt needed improvement. Daniel helped a lot with that by just being a good example. He rarely complained, while I tended to often. He was there when anyone needed him and was an example to all. I learned through him that I didn't have to always speak out on every thought or thing I disagreed with, or take things as personally as I did, or be quick to anger. I was realizing that the more attention I gave to things, the more power I gave it. I've learned that there are some things we just need to ignore or let go of for the sake of our own peace of mind. Through Daniel's example, I was learning what it meant to be humble, and the good that it could do for me.

21

Incredible India!

It was now summertime, and I had two weeks of vacation. I decided to visit my friend Natasha whom I had met at graduate school in Australia. It was my first time visiting India, and I was so excited that I couldn't sleep. Michael and I decided that we would meet there to explore together. When I arrived in India and stepped out of the airport, I knew instantly that this would be a life-changing experience. It was like the chaos of China and Egypt combined. For the first time on my journey, I felt a bit scared. I wasn't sure how I would survive such chaos! The stifling heat combined with the incessant honking of car horns had my head spinning. I had arranged everything via internet prior to my arrival, so I was picked up by my taxi driver at the airport. We immediately drove towards my hotel. Once again, my head was in my hands with all the cars, rickshaws and motorists who seemed to be driving right at each other. It did not seem like there were any lanes. It was like one big road without any signs. I was convinced that I would either be heading back home paralyzed or in a coffin. My cab driver was an older man who was friendly and polite. He had a lot of questions and was amazed that I was traveling alone. He thought it was courageous of me to come to India all by myself. However, when he dropped me off at my hotel, he turned towards me and said, "You're a smart girl, I think you will be just fine here."

The following day, I embarked on my four hour road trip to see the Taj Mahal. I was also going to meet up with Michael later that day. On our way, I couldn't ignore all the things that were happening around me. There is a wild disorder in India that is scary, yet so inviting. I had never experienced anything like it. I was drawn into all the activities that were happening all at once. People were selling goods by the road side; men were trying to tame an elephant that was blocking traffic in the streets, little kids kept knocking on the car window begging for money, young boys were playing soccer with a can, all with the never ending sound of cars honking. It was so much chaos, but within that chaos, there was a sense of order that I had never witnessed before. No one seemed disturbed by everything that was happening around them, it seemed like just another day in India!

We then stopped by a small shop to buy some drinks. I saw a little girl about six years old standing outside the shop in her underwear carrying a baby in her arms. Her brother who was a little older kept pushing her towards me. She was refusing to approach me and kept shrugging herself. He then turned around and slapped her so hard in the face that she started to cry. I became so enraged with emotions. There were people around, but no one said anything. I walked up to him and said firmly, "why did you hit her? You shouldn't hit other people, it's not right!" He responded in his Indian accent, "she is my sister, I can hit her, and she needs to listen to me!" I asked him why did he hit her, and he said that she was being disobedient to him and wouldn't ask me for money so they could eat. I asked him for his parents, and he said he didn't know. I kept rubbing my hands on the little girls back while she cried in the lap of her baby sister. I told her that it was ok, and that her brother didn't mean to hurt her, he didn't know better. Her brother stood there with his innocent eyes and looked remorseful. I was angry at him, but I wanted to hold him in my arms also. I wished I could take them all home with me. They were simply innocent kids trying to survive in a harsh world. Life can be so unfair.

My cab driver came out of the shop right when I was handing them some money to get lunch. He tried to stop me from giving it to them. He said that I would be running into hundreds of children like them every day, and usually it's all an act to get money from tourists. I felt like he was being very cold and unkind. I gave them the money anyway, and we proceeded on our journey. On the way, I saw poverty that I had never witnessed before. There was a certain stench in the air that made one feel like they constantly needed a bath. There were more naked children roaming the streets, and it seemed like a never ending stretch of poverty. I noticed one thing about the people in India; amidst all the poverty and chaos, most of them were always smiling. They are some of the most pleasant and happy people that I've ever met. Mother Teresa was right when she said that there is so much we can learn from the poor.

When we arrived at our hotel, I checked in, and then went out to explore my surroundings. I could see the peak of the Taj Mahal from my room, but I wasn't going to explore it until Michael arrived. Agra looked similar to everything that I had seen on my drive, but more intense. Later on, Michael arrived with his sister and we spoke about our discoveries since arrival. We were all amazed by the order that derived from the chaos around us and how happy everyone seemed despite it all. Things were a bit awkward at first since Michael's sister was not very happy with me. She was not pleased with my decision to not move to Sweden, and thought that I was being selfish. At dinner that night, they both expressed their displeasure with my decision not to move. She then told me that everything in love is a risk and that if I really loved her brother that I would take a risk. I was disappointed in her attitude towards me because of my choices, and felt that as a woman she should have understood how difficult a decision it was to have to give up my independence completely. Ironically, a few years later she was placed in the same situation in her relationship where she was being forced to choose by her partner to move to his hometown, and her first response was, "he expects me to give up my life to move with him to a place where I have no friends, family, or job?" It was then that I realized that some women like giving other women advise that they don't take or apply to themselves. I often question why is it so much easier for us to tear each other down than to provide encouragement and support. Throughout our discussion at dinner, I felt pressured, but didn't allow it to spoil my vacation.

We had a wonderful dinner, and even had our palms read by an in-house astrologer. His reading was a little amusing; he said that within the next year that I would be married and pregnant. It sounded a bit farfetched, as it was mid-year, and although I was engaged, we did not have a date for a wedding and I didn't see how I would have gotten pregnant within that time. I quickly dismissed the thought, but it did linger somewhere in the back of my mind. The following day we went to see the Taj Mahal. At first, it seems like its hidden away behind a great wall, but then you walk right into it and it immediately takes your breath away. There is something so magical and magnificent about this great work of art. It captivates you and draws you in. It looks like an image of something I had seen in my dreams. Almost like what I envision God's house to look like. I was in total awe, and knew right away that this would probably be the most fascinating thing that I would ever see in my lifetime.

We explored the beautiful building inside and out which surprisingly is well preserved for its age. We took lots of pictures, including the one on my book cover. I believe that how I was feeling in that very moment manifested itself in the photo and it continues to be one of my favorite memories. It was India's 60th Anniversary of Independence, and it marked a special day not just for India, but for me. This was one of the happiest moments in my life, a dream come true. We experienced a few more amazing sites, and by the end of the night we were thoroughly exhausted. Things were still tense between Michael and me, but I could sense how the stress of us being apart was taking a toll on him. He decided then to end our relationship. It was in that moment that I realized that I would have to make a decision. I agreed then to move to Sweden after my contract was up in a few months. Everything was ok from that moment.

We did some more exploring over the next couple of days, and then Michael and his sister flew to the city of Goa to relax on the beaches. I then flew to Mumbai to meet up with my friend Natasha and enjoy the rest of my vacation. I would meet up with Michael later on in Mumbai. Mumbai was a multiplied version of Agra in terms of chaos. Thankfully, I was prepared for it after being in Agra. I went to Natasha's house and stayed with her family for the remainder of my vacation. It was a privilege being able to experience the culture from a local perspective. Natasha's family was very hospitable, and I was getting a first-hand taste of what it was like living in India. They were upper middle class, so it was interesting to see the differences in culture. It was wonderful seeing Natasha again. We had spoken about this visit from way back when we were in Australia, and we never thought that it would actually happen. We were both excited about catching up on each other's lives.

A few days later, we flew to Udaipur to explore a different side of India. Udaipur was a more laid back, quiet city, with historical ruins which Natasha loved. It was a welcome relief to get away from the confusion of Mumbai and see a more scenic side of India; its lush vegetation, open fields, and a more relaxed lifestyle.

There was not as much poverty as in Mumbai and Delhi. People seemed a lot more relaxed and at peace with life. On my drive to a few local sites, I saw children walking home from school neatly dressed in their school uniforms. It reminded me of my days growing up in Saint-Lucia. The tourists would always stop and take pictures of us. I always wondered why they were so fascinated with us dressed in uniforms, until I grew up and realized how unique it was and how much it spoke of one's culture. I stopped and took a picture with them, while admiring their neatly combed heads. I continued on my journey enjoying the refreshing breeze on my face; while I talked and laughed with my dear friend. We went on a camel ride together which was scary, but a lot of fun. We then went to a restaurant to eat local Indian foods with our hands. Sometimes, it all seemed like a dream that I would be waking up from at any minute.

We spent a few days in Udaipur and returned to Mumbai where I met up with Michael and did some more exploring. I felt a lot closer with him on this trip because I had opened up to him in a way I never had before. I told him that I needed him in my life and wanted to share my life with him and was willing to move to Sweden. It had been a rollercoaster of ups and downs with the distance and various other challenges, but somehow we had managed to overcome it all. I always admired his persistent determination in getting what he wants. He went after what he wanted, and he was one of the few people I knew that I could always count on. I had come to understand from personal experiences what my grandfather said to me many years before; about what a man says and what a man does are two completely different things. Most men who were in my life, including my father had disappointed me, so it was always important to me to share my life with someone who was loyal, trustworthy and kept to their word. I was not looking over his imperfections, but I was focusing on his unique qualities that were genuine, rare and beautiful. I learned that when we truly love someone, it does not mean we overlook their flaws, it means that we know that like us, they are not perfect, and what they need and seek is for someone to love them anyway. In the end, we all just want to feel loved and feel that we matter.

22

Change Is Inevitable.

I returned to Japan feeling brand new. My journey to India felt like a spiritual one. One that was needed and vital. There is something about India that taps into one's level of consciousness. Your mind becomes over-stimulated by the concentration of contrasting images, sounds, and emotions and you feel a heightened sense of awareness. Witnessing so much life at once--- beauty, tragedy, hardship, happiness, laughter, struggle--- one feels completely tuned-in to the world outside, as well the world within you, and more alive than ever before. I returned to work with much enthusiasm and a different focus than I had before. I embraced the differences in culture a lot more, and was more receptive to change. My students always brought a smile to my face. I'm sure my presence added some color to their world, but the meaning and depth that they added to mine was so much more than I could have ever given them. I met some wonderful people in Japan and together we made our experience a memorable one. We were Australians, Canadians, Americans, South Africans, and English, and collectively we enriched each other's worlds with fun and laughter while we immersed ourselves in the Japanese lifestyle.

While it was always great meeting other people from other races and cultures, one thing I missed on my journey was seeing more people of color exploring unfamiliar territories and stepping outside of their comfort zones. In almost every group, I was usually the only black girl, and people were always fascinated that "a girl like me" would be so far from home and living such an unconventional life. As wonderful and rewarding as the experience was, I missed sharing, seeing and interacting with people of my own race and of similar culture. Rarely did I ever come across people of my race in my own age group at school, work, or even on vacation.

In Japan, I met an African-American woman named Reesha who was a Gunnery Sergeant/E-7 in the Marine Corps. I saw her in a restaurant with some friends one day, and Michael walked up to her and asked her where was she from and mentioned that I had been looking for people who looked like me in Japan for a while. We all had a good laugh and joked about being only a numbered few. She and I developed a friendship and she became a mentor to me. I admired her strength and her leadership. She had been serving in the U.S army for many years and worked her way up to a position of leadership and responsibility. She inspired me to keep striving and wanting to succeed. Every time I spoke with family and friends I tried to encourage them to broaden their horizons by challenging themselves to explore new places and cultures. Most of my friends were fascinated by my courage to travel the world as if it was impossible for them to do the same thing. I was once trying to convince a friend to accompany me on a journey, and she complained about how expensive the flights were. I sarcastically remarked that the trip was cheaper than her hand bag! We all have priorities in life, and I've learned that some people value material things a whole lot more than their own personal development.

    As time went by, I continued to write and share my pictures and journals with my friends about my experiences in Japan. One thing I never gave up doing on my journey was writing. Writing has always been my source of peace and happiness, and the best way I connect with others. My blog grew larger and attracted many people who started looking forward to my updates. I was my happiest when I was sharing my experience and journey with them. Although i was more open and candid than most people would be, it connected me with a wide range of people who appreciated and embraced me for simply being myself. That was the greatest gift that I could ever ask for. I have failed at many things in my life, none so hopelessly as when I was not being myself. Since then I haven't known how to be anything else.

    When we were in India, Michael and I had agreed that I would move to Sweden after my one year contract in Japan was up. I thought that it was a fair compromise, and was preparing yet again for the transition. However, soon after I returned from India, he started to express his frustration with us being apart and that I should move before my contract was over. While I was prepared to move to

Sweden, I wanted to at least complete my contract. I always try to do the right thing, and I thought that it was not fair to end my contract earlier simply because my boyfriend was being impatient. We spent weeks arguing about it, and slowly the pressure started taking a toll. I started to feel depressed, and had lost all enthusiasm for being in Japan. I wanted to have the encouragement and support of the person I loved, and I didn't feel like I was getting it. It placed me in a tough situation yet again, and I couldn't figure out how I would balance the two.

    Earlier that year, Michael had started his own business, and the stress and responsibility that came with it sometimes put a strain on our relationship .He said that he needed me by his side at such an important stage in his life, and that I should move to Sweden as soon as possible. I started to feel an enormous sense of guilt not being able to be there with him to support him and go through the process with him. It became even harder to try to convince him that waiting the four months for my contract to be complete was the best thing. Everything started to weigh on me. I hated feeling like I had to choose once again. Ultimately, I succumbed to the pressure and resigned from my position. I can remember writing to my mom about my decision. I knew she would be disappointed, and when I spoke to her, I could hear it in her voice.

    My mom's blessing on everything I did was always important to me. It hurt me to hear the sadness and disappointment in her voice. I think she knew that I would be giving up a major part of my independence which was very important to me. I can remember speaking with my friend Daniel about my feelings towards Michael's attitude about me moving to Sweden immediately. I told him that I thought that Michael was being selfish and that often times I had to adjust my life to accommodate his, and I didn't think that he was willing to do the same. But things were too complicated now to go back. We had already endured so much, and he had been there for me in many ways. He had made it his personal goal to continue making my dreams of traveling the world a reality. He had believed and supported me when I needed him, and I felt a strong sense of loyalty towards him. I thought maybe it was time for me to be more selfless, and that I needed to compromise. Although I spent the last weeks in Japan questioning my decision, I was looking forward to starting my new life with Michael. Deep down, I thought that my decision to move would be better for both of us. The ride to Narita airport from Gotemba was a long one. I knew that this was a life-changing decision, and that my life would never be the same.

23

New Beginnings.

I arrived in Sweden on a cold and windy day in October. I was greeted with flowers by Michael and he was very enthusiastic about my arrival. I loved that about him; he always did everything within his power to make me feel special and loved. Everything was already prepared for me when I got home, so settling into my new life started to feel right. As the days went by we established a routine for ourselves, and eagerly started planning towards our future. We started talking and making plans for our wedding the following year. Since we were from two different cultures and our families were on two different continents, deciding on a location posed a problem. We agreed on a small wedding, but like any girl, it was my first time and I wanted it to be really special. I always had a vision of what I wanted my day and dress to be like. Michael, who is Catholic, had been married before, so the option for a church wedding was out. Also, since he had a large wedding the first time around, he was not keen on anything big this time. This seemed to have been a reoccurring theme in our relationship. Michael was eleven years older than me, so some of the things I had yet to experience and was excited about he had a "been there, done that" attitude towards. Planning our wedding was already proving to be a clash of many things: age, geography, culture, religion, etc., but we had already defied the odds, so we were determined to stick with each other.

One month after moving to Sweden, I found out that I was pregnant! I guess the astrologer's predictions were right after all! Michael was in his late thirties and felt like it was time for him to become a father, and although I would have been happy to have waited a few more years to become a mother, I understand that relationships are about compromise, so we welcomed the surprise and was excited about having our first child. Michael wanted to become a father before the age of forty, and since he was thirty nine at the time, it was a wonderful gift. Being pregnant brought about a sense of relief. I was now able to focus on my new life in Sweden, and not feel compelled to choose between my career and relationship. Pregnancy made that transition easier, and allowed me to focus on my new role of soon to be wife and mother. Since I had gotten pregnant sooner than we expected, we decided that we didn't want to wait to get married and have Matthew outside of wedlock, so we decided we would elope. Suddenly, everything seemed to be happening very quickly. We were in the process of planning for a vacation to South Africa when I found out that I was pregnant, so we decided that we would get married in South Africa.

South Africa had always been a dream destination for both of us, and since I was not able to have the wedding of my dreams, Michael wanted to make it memorable for me in every way. A few weeks into my pregnancy, I started having terrible morning sickness. I was also feeling the stress and pressure of all the changes at once. One of the things I dreaded most was telling my mom that I was pregnant. I knew deep down that she would not only be surprised, but also a bit disappointed. I knew that she would have wanted me to be a lot more stable in my career before having a child. It was one of the most difficult calls that I ever had to make in my life. When I was six weeks pregnant, I decided to tell her. My first words were, "I have something to tell you," and she jokingly responded, "What, you're pregnant?" and when I responded yes, she screamed out "Are you serious?" She was in total disbelief. I think she always felt that marriage and family would come later on, and it was not something that was in my short term plans. I never shared my willingness to be a mother in the immediate future with her. She had such high hopes and expectations for me in terms of career and I didn't want to let her down.

There were a few seconds of silence, and then she congratulated me and teased me about the type of mother I would be. Although for the remaining conversation she was enthusiastic and supportive, I could sense the sadness in her voice. When I hung up the phone I cried. I always wanted my mother's blessing in everything I did. I always wanted to make her proud. I felt a huge responsibility to do so throughout my life. I felt like I had let her down. Still, it was a happy moment in my life, and I thought that it was probably the time to let go of my mother's hand and influence in my life, and now I could start listening to my own voice. At times, I felt caught up in the two worlds of trying to please my mother and Michael, since they both had their own expectations. It was hard to create a balance. Throughout the planning of our wedding in South Africa, I told no one of our plans to elope. I knew that my mother would not be thrilled with the idea, so I didn't say anything until right before we left. Again, she sounded disappointed, and I couldn't blame her, but I avoided lengthy conversations so we couldn't discuss it further. My heart ached at hearing the sadness in my mom's voice. I felt like I was moving on with my life and was excluding the person who meant the most to me in the entire world. She was always the most influential and most powerful presence in my life, and at the most important time in my life, I felt like she was absent. A lot of it was because of my own doing and wanting to avoid conflict between she and Michael. A few weeks later, we left for South Africa. It was just Michael and I and our baby growing inside of me.

24

It's A Long Walk To Freedom.

There is something about South Africa that captures you upon arrival. Perhaps it's the depth and history of its people and what they have endured and overcome. You can feel the enchanting spirit of their hero Nelson Mandela lingering in the air. Driving through Cape Town on the way to the condo we would be renting, I had goose bumps. This was one of my dream destinations growing up, and I could hardly believe that I was in this amazing place where I had watched my hero walk through the streets twenty years before with a raised fist chanting and singing songs of freedom. I felt an intense feeling of gratitude that I was able to experience this. Michael and I were amazed by how modern the city was. It looked like any major city in the U.S. It was very different from the images of Africa that we are usually bombarded with on television. There wasn't a naked, starving child or mud hut in sight. We drove along the scenic coastline on our way to the condo, and for a moment it seemed like I was driving through Malibu California. "Is this really South Africa?" I kept asking myself in disbelief. The abundance of beauty and variety of the landscape that surrounded me was more than I ever imagined. We were both happy that we had chosen this wonderful destination to get married. Everything about it is what dreams are made of.

Over the next few days we did a lot of exploring all over Cape Town. Every day, we found something new to marvel at and enjoy. The large open plains, vast stretches of beach and picturesque wineries made our daily drive an absolute pleasure. Some days were tougher than others for me despite how beautiful everything was. I was six weeks pregnant, and my morning sickness was terrible. My body was going through changes that even I couldn't understand. One day I would be overjoyed and feeling on top of the world, the next completely sad and crying my eyes out. It took away from enjoying every experience, because I was sometimes too tired or sick to take it all in. But, I was determined to make the best of it, and do everything we had planned for our vacation. We had everything arranged before we arrived, and every day there was a surprise from Michael. One day we would be touring the city of Cape Town from the skies in a private helicopter, then the next enjoying a safari with some of the most fascinating wild life, then diving with great white sharks, and then enjoying some of the most exquisite cuisines that we had ever tasted. Our condo was along the scenic coastline, so it was a pleasure waking up every day to the beautiful sunrise and blue waters.

One of the most memorable parts of the trip for me was visiting the prison cell of Nelson Mandela on Robben Island where he spent eighteen years of his life. On the ferry to get to the island, I sat in silence thinking of the many days and nights that he had to endure on this cold, isolated rock. I thought of his struggle and how much he and his family had to sacrifice to win their freedom and the freedom of others. This was an opportunity I was extremely grateful for, and I savored every bit of it. I wanted to take in every moment and keep it with me for as a long as I lived. Standing outside Mr. Mandela's small cell, I imagined him sitting on the concrete floor with nothing but hope and faith to keep him going. I thought of how empty and lonely his days must have been. I can only imagine the mental and physical pain that he had to endure, but he was still able to survive. He is a true testament of the power of the human spirit! I'm happy that he lived to tell his story and to see his dream become a reality.

Michael and I walked around Robben Island holding hands, and I felt an immense feeling of love for him that I hadn't felt for any man before. One rooted in gratitude and appreciation. When we first met, I told him of my admiration and love for Nelson Mandela, and my dream of visiting Robben Island one day. It became his dream too, and he did everything in his power to make it happen for me. He made sure everything went perfectly, and I could see the satisfaction in his eyes when I was overwhelmed with tears of joy. I was so thankful to have found someone who I thought was genuinely interested in my happiness. I had never met anyone, a part from my mother, who went above and beyond to make me happy and bring a smile to my face. He hated when I was sad or disappointed. He always wanted to do everything to make me happy, sometimes even more than he could. At times, it did feel like my Cinderella story, and in moments like these, I felt like the luckiest girl in the world. He always demanded and wanted the best for me, and would always remind me to demand the same for myself. This was one of the most valuable lessons I learned from sharing my life with him. To always demand the best of and for myself.

As the days went by, we were also busy preparing for our wedding. Everything was moving along smoothly since we hired a wedding planner to organize everything. Although everything was going as planned, there were stressful days which caused intense arguments between Michael and me. I couldn't stop thinking about not having my family there to share the day with me, especially my mother. I wanted to pick up the phone and call my mom and share every detail with her about my trip, but I knew that when I heard the sadness in her voice, I wouldn't be able to handle the guilt, so I opted not to. Sometimes when I tried to talk about how I felt with Michael, his attitude was cold and uncaring. He sometimes made me feel ungrateful for complaining when he was doing everything to make it a perfect day for me. His attitude made me realize how selfish and controlling he can be. I did not understand how he could think that I would not be sad in not having my mother by my side, or my family and friends to share this special moment. He said this was a part of life, and that my mother had too much control and influence in my life, and that my focus should be on my own family now. Observing his lack of understanding and empathy towards the situation started to really concern me, but I couldn't overlook all the wonderful things he had done and ways that he had shown his love, and thought maybe he was right; perhaps I was spending too much time and focus on what was wrong and missing, and needed to focus on my blessings. After all, we had both agreed that we would later renew our vows and have a ceremony for our family, so I thought that we would be able to celebrate then.

I decided to no longer make it an issue, and spent the rest of the time preparing for my big day. I did a lot of reflection while in South Africa. I was about to take one of the biggest steps in my life, and was going to be a mother for the first time in just a few months. They were two of the most important events in my life. I always thought that it was ok to fail at anything in life, but not at being a mother. I saw motherhood as a privilege, and an absolute blessing. It is something that God entrusts us with, and I did not want to let him and myself down. My mom had six children and she tried her best. She led by example, and she did everything to ensure that we grew up to be good, well-mannered, disciplined and good-hearted individuals. I wanted all this and more for my child as well. All my life, it seemed that I was searching for something greater than me, and I tried to define life on my own terms. I made no apologies for that, but a lot of my decisions were made with mainly me and my best interests in mind. Perhaps, that was not a bad thing. I was still relatively young, and like everyone else, trying to understand who I am and why I was placed in this world. But, it came with a lot of instability. I was often indecisive and found it difficult to give all of myself and commit to anyone. I was ready for that stability that I felt was missing. I had reached a place in my life where I was willing to sacrifice my own happiness and ambitions to be there for someone else. I was willing to do that for my son, and the man I would be marrying, even with his imperfections, he had proven to me that he was worthy of my love.

    When we woke up on the morning of our wedding it was one of the most beautiful days of our vacation. I didn't have the morning sickness that had been plaguing me throughout the trip. I felt like a princess in my dress. Michael looked like a prince in his tailored suit, and it was hard to take my eyes off of him. We had a small legal ceremony in a mansion at a friend's house in the hills of Cape Town. Our friend Simon's family and friends served as witnesses. It was a beautiful house with large open windows which provided a wonderful view of the well cared for grounds of the estate with all its colorful flowers and lush vegetation. The weather was perfect, and the entire atmosphere was filled with laughter, tears of joy and the sound of our wedding song by Freddie Jackson, "All I ever ask," serenaded us throughout. We were then picked up in a Rolls Royce and driven to the famous Table Mountain where we exchanged vows. Our driver escorted Michael and me out of the car and we then walked me to take the cable lift to get to the top of the mountain. Tourists who came to visit the famous mountain took pictures, cheered and congratulated us as we walked by. I felt like a celebrity as I waved and thanked them. The view from the Table Mountain is one of the most breathtakingly beautiful views that I've ever seen. Beyond the impressive cliffs, the city of Cape Town is sprawled out, surrounded by the Atlantic Ocean with Robben Island visible in the distance. As we stood on the plateau of this World Heritage Site and exchanged our vows, we spoke from the heart, and were both emotional. It was a wonderful moment for both of us. I felt connected with my husband in every way, and I couldn't wait to continue sharing my life with him and our baby growing inside of me.

After we exchanged vows, we drove along the winding roads to a beautiful winery to have a romantic dinner. On the drive to the winery, I started to feel sick, and began to vomit. It took a lot of my energy and excitement away, but soon after I felt better, and we were able to complete the day enjoying our candle light dinner and reminiscing on our day. We had come a long way from where we began. Almost two years after meeting, we became husband and wife. At times it tested everything within us, and we were forced to learn the true art of compromise, but we always seemed to find our way back to each other. We were now expecting our first child, and it was a new chapter in our lives. It was one that we were excited about and anxiously anticipating. Sadly, our trip to South Africa had come to an end. It was difficult to leave, since it was one of the most memorable and life-changing times of my life. It remains my favorite destination, and is a place that I hope to visit again one day.

25

Life Feels Empty When You Are Existing And Not Living.

    As much as I loved South Africa, it was great to be in Sweden again, to get back into the routine of things. We were now married and pregnant, so our focus was on creating a solid foundation for our family. Michael was very busy with running his own floor sanding business, and I spent my days adjusting to my new role as a housewife. I was unable to work or go to school for a few months while I awaited my permanent residency in Sweden, so I had more time on my hands than I was used to. This took some adjusting to as I was used to always working towards a goal and juggling many things at once, but I quickly learned to adapt to the routine of being a housewife and a support system for my husband. It was a new role I embraced as I anxiously prepared for all the wonderful changes that waited on the horizon. We were getting ready to move into our brand new home in a new neighborhood, and were eagerly awaiting the birth of our baby. It was a fresh start. I was optimistic about all the possibilities ahead and loved that I could be there to help in building a solid and stable foundation for our family.

    A few months later, we moved from Michael´s apartment in the city into our home outside the city. It was nestled in the middle of nature with lots of trees and greenery surrounding it, which is something that Sweden is known for---its vast forests and unspoiled natural beauty. Our house was not a mansion, but it was our first home together, and we loved it. It was the first time that either of us owned a home, so we felt like it was our new beginning. We both worked at designing it to add our own personalities and tastes to make it one that we enjoyed living in. The neighborhood was an exclusive one with affluent neighbors who seemed to work hard at trying to outdo each other with nicer lawns, cars, and fencing. At first we loved that everyone took such pride in their homes and that we were surrounded by people who had high standards, but the atmosphere of competition eventually got a bit tiring, and took away from the community spirit, which seemed counter to a collective society like Sweden which is all about everyone living on the same level.

On most days, I enjoyed taking my usual morning walks and looked forward to being outside, which was always so tranquil and peaceful. I even loved the silence and the fact that there were very few people. I spent hours outdoors just being at one with nature; reading, writing, and talking to my baby growing inside of me. For a while, it felt like home, and I was happy, but I've learned that too much of anything, no matter how good, is not always a good thing. With every passing day, I was learning a lot more about Sweden and its unique culture, and I was beginning to realize that life in Sweden would require a lot more patience and strength than I anticipated. Sweden is a quiet and peaceful country. The people are shy and reserved and keep to themselves, so it was not easy integrating into the culture and making friends. They are polite, but not the friendliest and they tend to set up boundaries which make it very difficult for anyone to get past the level of polite friendliness. Michael and I were both immigrants, and although he had been living there for twenty years, he always considered Poland to be his home. However, because of his work, he settled in Sweden. He had one sister who also lived in Sweden who he spent most of his time with, so he rarely integrated and had few friends, which made our network small. At first, it was very difficult for me to understand how he could live there and not mix with Swedes, but as I assimilated more into the culture, I learned that the structure of society alienates immigrants and causes division between them.

Most Swedes live in their own worlds and immigrants in theirs. Many immigrants find it difficult to call it home no matter how long they live there, because they rarely feel included or accepted. As a social butterfly and a lover of people, this was one of the biggest challenges for me. It was very hard to make eye contact with others much less get them to engage in a conversation, and if you do, they say very little which often makes the conversation seem like a monolog, and a bit uncomfortable. In Sweden, one is taught not to stand out, or to showcase their knowledge and intelligence.

This is seen as bragging or not being humble. Because of this, immigrants are often categorized as people who are not humble and like to talk about themselves. It is hard for immigrants to create a balance with this, because if you share a lot of information about yourself to get conversations going, then it is seen as bragging, but if you ask them a lot of questions about themselves, it is considered intrusive, and if you say nothing there is no conversation. Since almost all Swedes speak English well, it was easy to find my way around, but it made it hard to learn the already difficult language. And since most of them barely spoke, one had few chances to practice with others. One of the biggest adjustments in Sweden is that no matter where you come from, to get any form of employment you must know how to speak the language, even though almost all Swedes speak and understand English well. For most careers, you are required to go back to school and get the Swedish qualifications before you are offered a job.

Finding employment would still be almost impossible for any immigrant with or without Swedish qualifications unless one was willing to settle for jobs such as shopkeepers, store clerks, cleaners, and other jobs that required no academic qualifications. A government agency called *abertsfedmedling* is responsible for finding employment for everyone, and their success rate is almost non-existent. Unless an immigrant is hired by an organization and brought to Sweden by them, finding employment aligned with one's qualifications is almost impossible. This was one of the biggest setbacks for me, and something that really worried me. I knew that it would take time to assimilate into the culture and find a job, but I didn't think that I would have to settle and even change my entire life because of Socialism. One thing that you can count on in Sweden however, is being able to receive an education because it is free! Unfortunately, most immigrants often become professional students and are forced to over-embrace Sweden's lifelong learning concept, because they can't find a job in their respective fields.

Before moving to Sweden, I was aware that it was a Socialist country, however, I did not have an understanding of the depth and history of socialism. It is engrained in their culture, thinking and way of life. For immigrants living in the country, it often requires some getting used to, especially if one is coming from a more capitalistic society. However, most immigrants adapt, but find it difficult to conform to the Swedish way of doing things. Because of its geographic location, it is dark, cold, and rainy for almost nine months of the year, with very little sunlight. By the end of November, the nights are eighteen hours long, but on a brighter note, in the summer time, the sun does not set until 11pm and rises at about 4am! At first, I didn't understand when Michael said that Swedes personalities had a lot to do with their lack of sunlight. I never realized how vital sunshine is to our lives until moving to Sweden, but after living there for a few years, I was fighting to maintain my enthusiasm for life and not let a frown be a permanent sign on my face.

All these new harsh realities caused me to have a very low morale and confirmed most of the fears I had before moving. There is a type of darkness in Sweden that I've never experienced anywhere else, both literally and figuratively. In the eyes of many around the world, Sweden is seen as the ideal place to live and raise families, and is admired for its progressive attitude, culture of tolerance and humanitarian work for the thousands of refugees it takes in every year, but when you live there you learn to understand like everything else in life, it comes at a hefty price. For immigrants you are almost forced to give up your identity to be able to live there. There are many things I loved about living in Sweden; its rugged, yet tranquil natural beauty, its ability to preserve its culture despite the changes in the world, its unwavering commitment to children, health care, and a stable way of life for all. But as time went by however, I was learning what was meant by "existing and not living." I was beginning to feel with each passing day that I had this perfect life, but I was simply existing and not living.

26

Life Is Art.

Despite the cultural differences and difficulty assimilating into the culture, I did everything within my power to make Sweden feel like home. I started to marvel at the white snow that sat on my window pane, instead of feeling confined by it. I remembered how excited I got as a child at the sound of rain drops on my galvanized metal roof, and would put on my rain boots and walk in the rain instead of allowing it to dampen my spirit. I always loved my own company, so I embraced being alone often. I was still amazed by where my imagination could take me. I had decided that Sweden was my new home and I was determined to make the best of it. Within a few months, I had become a permanent resident and was attending classes to learn Swedish. I was having a very easy pregnancy, and Michael was an overprotective husband who treated me more like an invalid than a pregnant woman for fear of anything that could go wrong. There were more wonderful days of relaxation and bliss by the lake. Still, I had this emptiness inside me that nothing seemed to fill. I found happiness in things temporarily, and would always revert to a solemn and sad state. I knew Michael could see the unhappiness and emptiness in my eyes. He tried everything to help me adjust to my new life and make it a comfortable one for which I was extremely grateful, but this void I felt just didn't seem to go away. I couldn't understand it, especially since I had everything I had always dreamed of as a child---a family, new home and a good life.

My morale was low, and I found very little motivation to do anything. I wasn't even interested in learning Swedish. I was often tired and slept a lot. I thought perhaps it was the symptoms of pregnancy and it would eventually go away. I would do everything to try to keep busy and keep my spirits up. I started many projects with enthusiasm, and would eventually lose focus and the zeal to continue. Sometimes I feared that I was turning into a "Swede" and I would become isolated and be confined to myself, so to help not lose touch with myself I did everything to stay in touch with my culture and people.

I was an active user of facebook, which I used to keep in touch with my family and friends and current affairs. It was a great escape from the isolation and loneliness in Sweden. As usual, I used writing as a way to express myself, and would often write about the things that I was passionate about. Michael is a lot more reserved and introverted, so I knew that my new life would definitely take some getting used to, but I felt like I had to change everything about myself to adapt to his life. Michael enjoyed doing everything together and having it always be just the two of us, while i believed in creating more of a balance, especially coming from the Caribbean with a close knit of family and circle friends. Nonetheless, I knew of this before we got married, and had learned to adjust to it. However, it was more intense now that we lived together and had to deal with it every day.

Before living together, it was easier to create balance because we were often apart. I welcomed the differences in our personalities, and wanted him to be himself, but it posed a problem when I wanted to be myself. It usually brought about arguments, so I slowly started changing that about me. I also learned quickly that our household would be a Polish one, so we celebrated most Polish traditions, and acknowledged its important days; none of that was done for my own country´s traditions. It made me feel like I was losing my identity in every way. The days started to feel very long. Michael was working long hours, and I spent a lot of time at home. Since I didn´t have any friends as yet, I spent most of my time alone. I spent the time being creative, writing, and corresponding with friends. There were days I found myself incredibly homesick, but I always found something to do to get my mind past it.

One day while surfing through facebook, I discovered the beautiful paintings of artist Jonathan Guy-Gladding. I was instantly mesmerized and captivated by his portrayal of Caribbean culture and people. He captured the beauty of my culture in a way that I had never seen which brought me back to my childhood days. I contacted him to inquire more about his work, and he responded with humility and grace. He had been a computer artist/animator when he decided to give it up and become a Peace Corps volunteer in Saint Lucia. In his spare time he would create paintings of the local people and culture. He realized his true passion and decided to focus on painting when his peace crop service was finished. He gave up his career and took a leap of faith by becoming an artist full-time.

He also decided to make Saint Lucia his second home, where he still lives and paints. I asked him what inspired him to give up a good job and serve in a developing country, and he said that he wanted to make a contribution to humanity. He said he wanted to experience a little hardship for something worthwhile and grow as a person in the process. He had had a fairly easy life and wanted to do something to give back to others. He had found a great sense of purpose and meaning by capturing the unique culture and people of Saint Lucia on canvas and preserving a special way of life that is being lost in so much of the world. It was one of the first times he felt like he was using his life for a greater good, by inspiring many with his God given talent and something he is passionate about. I admired his ability to be courageous enough to follow his dreams and do what he loved. I was impressed by his story, and it caused me to think of my life before I met Michael. I was on a similar journey where I wanted to use my life to help others and discover my true purpose, but I went off track. I thought that being married and pregnant would have filled that desire and allow me to forget about my dreams and aspirations, but I still yearned to fulfill that purpose. I felt an immediate connection with Jonathan's paintings, and his story seemed to have ignited something within me. It brought back memories of me as a child, and the dreams I had. Back then I was full of enthusiasm and vigor, curious, and optimistic about life and the things and people in it.

As a little girl, I wanted to see more and learn more of the world. I wanted to be like Barbara Walters and Oprah Winfrey. They were my "she-roes." I was fearless, and felt like I could do anything that I set my mind to, but slowly all this seemed to be fading away. I never had any appreciation for art, but through Jonathan's paintings I was learning just how much of our own life is art. His paintings tapped into my inner-child and ultimately answered the reason for this empty feeling inside. As much as one loves their partner, one also needs to have their own identity; their own life, family, friends, work, and all the other things that make them feel whole. I wasn't feeling whole. It was one of my greatest fears before moving to

Sweden, and it was proving to be right. Ironically, my encounter with Jonathan would be no coincidence, as he would later be a mentor in my life and encouraged me to speak my truth by sharing my story with the world.

27

You Can Only Find Yourself When You Lose Yourself.

My pregnancy was a smooth and easy one, but the experience seemed like an eternity. I felt like I had been pregnant for three years, especially since I wasn't as active as I usually am. However, I loved being pregnant. It was the time when I felt the most beautiful in my life. My hair was shining and my skin was glowing like never before. The feeling of a life growing inside of you is an indescribable one. A few months into my pregnancy I found out that we were having a boy. We were both thrilled. I always wanted to have four boys and vowed that one of them would be named Matthew. Surprisingly, Michael always thought that if he ever had a boy that he would name him Matthew after his brother who passed away, so long before he was born, we knew of his name and spoke to him all the time. He was our little angel, and we couldn't wait to hold him in our arms. I had a special bond with Matthew before I knew him. I talked to him every day and I knew that he could feel all the changes within me. There were days I would just sit in his room and pictured his face. I imagined what he would look, feel and smell like. It was a wonderful feeling; I could hardly wait to meet this precious angel.

As we eagerly waited to welcome our son into the world, we settled into our routine and tried to adjust to all the new changes in our lives. We started to realize how challenging it was to balance our worlds. Everything seemed to have come all at once, marriage, baby, new home, living together, new business for Michael, and me being a house wife. Sometimes it overwhelmed us having to deal with all these changes while trying to add to each other's happiness. At times it was very stressful for us especially since it was not an easy transition for me. One of the things that drew us to each other was our independent spirit and our desire to live our lives against convention. When we first met, Michael was a single thirty-something without children who loved his ability to live his life without borders, and I was a twenty-something just learning to spread my wings and wanting to fulfill all my heart's desires. We had met on the opposite side of the world while traveling alone with a huge appetite for life and discovering new places and people.

Michael was captivated by my fearless spirit and independence, and I loved his courage and curious nature. For two years, we had a long distance relationship where we traveled the world and discovered more about each other. Our curious natures and desire to explore the globe kept us connected even when living apart. Now that we were married and living the conventional life, it was a lot more challenging than we thought. Michael was going through changes too. Although he was ready to settle down and have a family, I think the reality of it all got a bit scary for him. He was now responsible for a family and sometimes he questioned if pressuring me to move to Sweden was the best decision, since he realized how much I struggled with it, and how unhappy I was at times. It was very hard for him to accept that there was nothing within his power that he could do to see that light in me again. I tried my best to hide it and be the best wife that I could be, but we both knew that there was a void that nothing seemed to fill. However, since we are both two persistent and committed people and understood that everything in life requires hard work, we were determined to get through those tests. We blamed it on the usual first year of marriage and the anxiety of pregnancy, and convinced ourselves that in time everything would fall into place. For a long time it did.

When Matthew came into the world, I instantly fell in love with him. Watching Michael holding our baby in his arms with tears of joy streaming down his cheeks is a picture that is burned into my memory forever. I could see how happy he was to be a father and how much he loved him. To us he was perfect. He was like everything I imagined and more, and sometimes it was hard to believe that he was all mine. It was a surreal feeling entering the hospital just the two of us, and leaving with another human being. It was also a scary feeling and we were praying that we wouldn't do anything wrong. We were first time parents and did not have the help of the extended family or friends as we were away from home, so although we were overjoyed, we were very nervous. The first few weeks were smooth sailing, and we were doting parents who spent every moment with our son. There were many times when we would just lay down next to him and watch him sleep. He was so beautiful and brought us so much joy. Our family now felt complete. For a while I was so consumed with motherhood that I slowly started to forget about the void that I had been feeling prior to Matthew's arrival. Matthew brought a light and joy into our lives and home that was needed, and we thought that he was the missing component to fill the emptiness that I had been feeling. We saw it as a transitional phase of marriage, and focused all our time and attention on being the best parents that we could be. Michael was instantly a nervous father which added even more pressure to the anxiety of being a mother for the first time. Although taking care of Matthew came as natural as breathing for me, it was sometimes stressful because of Michael's over protective nature. But, since i knew that he had waited a very long time to become a father, I was understanding of it.

    As the months went by, I embraced all the wonderful joys of being a mother. I looked forward to giving Matthew his baths, feeding him, singing and reading to him, changing him, putting him to sleep, taking long walks, and all the other wonderful things that make motherhood so beautiful. Michael and I loved watching him grow and looked forward to every step in his development. I can still remember the first sound he made, his first word, the first time he crawled, walked, and all the other wonderful firsts in his life. We were like children all over again as we took part in every activity in his life. There was so much laughter as his personality started to unfold. Sometimes when we were having a bad day, he could easily do something that brought smiles to our faces. One of the things that we promised ourselves was that we wouldn't give up on our love of traveling once Matthew was born, so we continued to travel the world with him from the time he was six weeks old. It was a challenge for us flying to countries as far as Mauritius and Argentina with an active baby, but he was almost always a great sport, and adapted to every country. Together, we saw some fascinating places and created memories for a lifetime.

    Fortunately Michael's business was doing really well. For years he had been working for someone else and had little to show for it. When we met, I suggested to him that he could do the same thing but have his own business and be his own boss. It took some convincing but we went ahead with the plan and in less than a year it was paying off. Swedes are a modest people without a lot of personal indulgences but they love wood, especially wood floors and were happy to pay for quality work, which Michael provided. Swedes also make few complaints and pay on time so they were ideal clients and business was booming. Michael and I didn't care about buying a lot of fancy things for ourselves but we were happy to spend the extra money we were earning to travel and feed our passion for seeing the world. And those trips were worth every kronor, not only for the experience of seeing other interesting places, but also to temporarily escape the dreariness and depressiveness of the Swedish winter.

However, once the novelty started to wear off, we were forced to face our harsh realities. I started to feel that emptiness inside creeping up on me again. Often our frequent vacations were an escape from the loneliness and isolation in Sweden. Parenting was exceptionally challenging for us because apart from not having the support from either of our families since they lived so far away, and living in a place that was not our home, it was cold, dark and grey. It's not easy raising a child in such an environment, especially when one has the odds stacked against them. There were times when the weather was so bad that out of sheer frustration, we would book a flight online and fly out within days. It was a good escape, but we always had to come back and face reality. On most days, Michael was working a lot, and it was often just Matt and I. As much as I enjoyed being a mother, it didn't fill up that emptiness inside. I think it even forced me to face it head on. I wrestled with that feeling often and felt an enormous sense of guilt. I knew that motherhood was the most important job of my life, and Matthew was the most important person in my life, yet, I still felt like I wasn't able to be the best mother to him, or the best person that I could be without feeling fulfilled, by doing something that made me feel like I was using my life, gifts, talents and skills in some meaningful way. In fact, it made me want to utilize these gifts even more. I wanted to create a balance in my life so I could be the best mother for my son. How could I be that if I wasn't truly happy?

Motherhood was especially challenging for me because I

couldn't share it with my family and friends. There was no one around, and aside from the random women I met every day while on the playgrounds or on my walks, I didn't have any friend or my mother nearby to share the experience with me, especially on the days when Michael was working a lot. I didn't talk about that much, because I didn't want it to seem like I was complaining about taking care of my son, because I wasn't complaining, but I knew that I would be judged or criticized by some mothers who often try to make other moms feel inadequate for reaching out. The irony is that they are often struggling with the same thing, but since they have been brainwashed by society into being "superwomen," and accept motherhood as some form of enslavement where women are not supposed to have a life outside of being a mother, they seldom complain. They often always wear a brave face, and feel guilty when they complain. I thought, how dare I complain when all I have to do was take care of my son? But that was the problem; it was all I had to do! I wanted and needed a balance. I wanted to have the support of an extended family. I wanted to be in a place where I was able to share the experience of motherhood with others. I wanted to celebrate my traditions with him also, and do the things that made motherhood fun. But, it was usually just he and I with rarely anything to do or anywhere to go. I never got a break. There was no one else to hold him to give me a minute for myself. It's so important to have the support of the extended family, which was how I was raised, because I believe that it really does take a village to raise a child.

It seems that the role of the extended family is slowly diminishing and is being replaced by an abbreviated family unit which consist of parents and a child who is overindulged and lavished with "things" and sadly doesn't learn to appreciate the simple things in life. I grew up not having much, but I appreciated the influence of my grandparents, aunts, uncles and the people in my community who gave structure to my life, and shaped me into the woman I am. There were days when I thought that I was going crazy. I would sit in the shower and just cry, or when he fell into sleep, I would pace around the house with things to do, but was feeling so lost that I just didn't do anything. I was slowly losing touch with myself. Sometimes I did not recognize the girl in the mirror. Every day felt and looked like the day before. It was the same routine, doing the same thing over and over again while feeling like I was slowly dying inside. It was hard to articulate that to Michael. He thought that this was the job of all mothers and I had nothing to complain about. He didn't help in absolving me of any guilt, in fact he would often make me feel worse when I expressed my feelings. The fact that I had a good life was enough, and how dare I complain. Soon, I started hearing less of that assertive voice and my independence was replaced with complete dependence on my husband. It made me feel even more helpless and empty inside. It opened the doors to all kinds of other issues in our marriage and made me lose touch with myself completely. I felt trapped, and I didn't know how to find my way back to me even if I tried. I was living in a foreign land without my family and friends, feeling depressed, confused, with a husband who didn't understand my pain, no job, and feeling like I was losing my mind. I felt totally helpless! I knew that I loved my son more than anything, but being a mother was not enough to make me feel whole. I believe that to be the best wife and mother that I could possibly be I needed to have my own identity and my own life. No one could fill that void for me. I needed to fill it on my own by feeling like I was in control of my own life.

28

Every ending Is An Opportunity For A New Beginning.

      For a long time, I went through each day trying everything I could to distract myself from having to deal with this empty feeling inside. I would try to think of every possible reason for why I could be feeling this way, and would often blame it on whatever new changes were taking place in our lives. For about two years, I tried to find a way to balance being a wife, mother, and attempting to have a career. Nothing I tried worked. My life was different now. Although there were opportunities, I was now married, with child, living on a different side of the world, so I had to consider many factors. Everything in life requires focus, and my focus and attention was centered on my family more than anything else. I did not mind that, but I didn't think that I would have to choose between having a career and having a family. Before we got married, Michael was always aware of my dreams and ambitions. He loved that about me, but it also concerned him. He worried that it would eventually take the focus away from our relationship and family. He would be supportive of me in doing something, but would also make me feel guilty for having those ambitions, so often times I felt like I had to choose. It got even worse after we got married. He would be supportive of my dreams, but it had to be within his narrow confines of what was best for our family.

      With every new venture, he made it more difficult for me to create that balance. He would always make me feel guilty for wanting to pursue my career and follow my dreams. The questions always led back to, "What about Matthew and I? How could you do this and balance our family life?" Everything seemed impossible! Yet, I never objected or questioned when he was pursuing his goals and dreams. I wanted to be a supportive and understanding wife. I thought that perhaps that this was the natural order of things--- that it is up to the woman to dedicate her life and focus all of her energies on her husband and family. But did it really have to be one or the other? Was it really impossible for me to utilize all my talents and education and still be a good mother and wife? I knew I could do both. I knew that my instincts as a mother and my love for my child would never allow me to deprive him any of the care and attention he needed, even while having other interests and personal goals. But, I felt like it was impossible to have a career now that I was a mother, unless it was convenient to Michael and Matthew.

I understood that my life was now different and sacrifices had to be made, but my life did not end when I got married and had a baby, in fact it seemed that it had just begun. I wanted more than ever to fulfill all the dreams and plans that I had for myself, and to create a balanced life for my family. It seemed to me that there was a power struggle. I think that Michael thought that once I became a wife and a mother that I would have given up on my dreams and settle into my new role. He continued to do everything he could to make it a comfortable life for me, and couldn't understand why it wasn't enough to make me feel fulfilled. I couldn't explain it either, but I knew that although I was thankful for all he did as the bread winner of our family, I was growing resentful toward him for attempting to change me and to keep me from reaching my full potential. I wanted him to support me the same way I supported him when he pursued his goals and dreams, but it didn't seem to be the same.

After many failed attempts at getting my career going, I decided that perhaps it was best if I did give up on my aspirations and settle for something that was convenient to my life in Sweden. I went back to school to get another degree in hopes of integrating into Swedish culture and finding a job. Everything seemed to be going fine, but when you're doing something against yourself, it's hard to find the focus or motivation. I had already gone to University for six years, and had no interest or desire to start all over again. It was not something that I was passionate about. It made me realize even more that I was on the wrong path. One day on my usual morning walk with Matthew, I looked around at my quiet, perfect neighborhood, and could hear nothing but the sound of my heavy breathing. My eyes flooded with tears and I started sobbing. I felt a depth of emptiness inside that I'd never felt before. I reflected on my life and where it had taken me. As a little girl, I dreamt of having the life I had. I thought it would define me, make me happy and signify my success. For the most part it did. I was proud of my accomplishments and the life that I had created for myself, but it came at a price a lot higher than what I was willing to pay.

There were times when I had to deny my own voice and compromise a great part of who I am only to discover that the answers I was searching for all along lived within me, and could be found if I had stayed true to my authentic self. I was great enough by just being me. I didn't have to prove anything to anyone. I looked back on my journey and realized that as much as I questioned convention and tried to define my own life, I still got caught up in the conventional way of doing things. I felt unworthy when I had little. I felt insignificant when I wasn't doing something that would impress others. I felt selfish when I wanted to focus on my goals and ambitions, and I would feel like a failure if i had reached a certain age and was not married and had a child. I had succumbed to the pressures of society, even when I was still trying to understand my own life and growing into my true self. I denied my inner voice, and I did what I felt I needed to do, to feel accepted, worthy and have a sense of belonging, but I ultimately lost touch with myself. Somehow, I got caught up in the trap of social acceptability and didn't know how to find my way back to me. I missed the girl who tried to define life on her own terms, and stayed true to her beliefs and convictions.

I was grateful for the life I had, and felt blessed for being given the opportunity to see the world and experience all its wonderful mysteries, but I was no longer willing to deny my voice and my happiness. I believe that if it looks good to the world but doesn't feel right in our hearts, then we are denying ourselves true happiness and the opportunity to reach our potential and be the person that we are meant to be. I was not willing to deny myself of that anymore. After three years of marriage, Michael and I decided to get a divorce. It was a decision that we wrestled with, because there were so many things that connected us, but it just wasn't enough to sustain us. We had both tried to find a way to work through the differences, but it had already divided us and tore us apart. I took one year after our divorce to spend with myself. Divorce is a painful process. It requires a great amount of strength and courage, and even when it's for the best, it feels like a death. It was the most difficult decision that I've ever had to make and one of the most difficult times of my life. I shared the news of my divorce only with my immediate family and closest friends, but never spoke of it with anyone again until now. I believe that when one is going through a difficult situation that it's important to take time to heal and get rid of all the things that can cause one to go even further from themselves.

While it's always good to talk to others, sometimes we are consumed with emotions that can alter our thought process and state of mind, and we can easily be influenced and manipulated by others thoughts and opinions. It's important for us not to allow our emotions to get the best of us, and create even more chaos and division. I didn't need to hear anyone's thoughts and opinions on my divorce, or felt the need to explain it to everyone either. This was between Michael and me. I've learned that sometimes there is no wrong or right answer. Sometimes the dots just do not connect and we have to learn to let go and be strong enough to know that we are capable of connecting the dots on our own. This was about evolving and growing into my own. In all major decisions in my life, I try to hear my own voice before anyone else's. I know that I am the only one responsible for my life and my decisions, and spending time alone provided much needed clarity and allowed me to realize my strength and my weaknesses. Through it all, I maintained a positive attitude and tried to be there for others also. It helped sustain me and kept me inspired. In life, we all want a happily-ever-after ending, which essentially gives us a goal to strive for, but we need to also know that there is happiness and fulfillment even when things don't go as expected or planned. Often happiness can be found simply in striving toward our goals and the knowledge that we are following our own compass. At the age of thirty one, if someone had told me that I would be divorced, a mother and writing my memoir, I would have doubted it. However, it's something that I've fully embraced. I've learned that every ending is an opportunity for a new beginning.

29

The Return To Me.

I´ve learned that it takes a lot of courage to grow up and be you- the person that God created and intended for you to be. Being oneself requires a whole lot of strength, determination and the ability to think with originality, especially since the world often tries to make us in the image of everyone else. What is the purpose of uniqueness if we all aspire to be the same? We are in constant pursuit of happiness, yet it continues to elude us, because we are forced to deny so much of our own truth and voice in the name of conformity and to make others happy. We walk around with masks on and rarely show how we truly feel. Meanwhile, there is a voice crying out inside wanting to be heard. We all have a yearning to represent ourselves in our own likeness and no one else´s. Life continues to evolve as it should, yet we remain fearful of change and wary of others. I´ve learned that one size does not fit all. Most of us attempt to express our individuality in whichever way we see fit, but are often pulled in varied directions by so many elements, which often causes us to feel lost and confused.

We have the tendency to associate success with strength and failure with weakness, when often it is after our mistakes and failures that we discover our strength. Why then do we condemn and criticize each other when we falter? How are we supposed to evolve and discover our true selves if we don´t embrace each other´s strengths and weaknesses and allow others to be themselves and speak their truths? Throughout my journey, I tried to search for the answers to some of life´s questions by stepping outside of my comfort zone and challenging my inhibitions. I wanted to learn more about life and others to gain an understanding of the world that we live in, and in the process, learn more about myself. Sometimes the answers were not what I anticipated or expected, and other times I did not receive any answer. Sometimes I went off track and even lost my way, but it was through all those changes and experiences that I was able to discover my true self. The hard times I went through may not have been fun, but they shaped my character and gave me strength and wisdom for the rest of my journey.

One of the most valuable lessons that I've learned from the wonderful places that I've seen and interesting people that I've met is that we are all students. We are all searching and yearning for someone or something to help make us better and push us to be the best that we can be. We all want to feel like we are a part of something greater and reach our full potential. It's what keeps us going and striving to be our best. Although we are whole and complete all on our own, no man can survive in this world alone. We all need each other and want to love and be loved, which is perhaps the greatest form of happiness. Without it, we are like empty vessels with a constant need to be filled and refilled. My curiosity took me even further than I imagined it could, and it provided a window into the world that I would have never known if I didn't allow myself the freedom to grow and embrace the beauty of change. Perhaps if I didn't pursue all my heart's desires then I wouldn't be able to articulate my struggles and triumphs with others.

I was inspired to write this book and speak my truth because I needed to feel liberated. Liberated from the restraints and boundaries that society has set up for us which cause us to live in a state of despair and disarray. We all struggle with the same things, yet we are taught to walk around with a brave face, afraid to show any sign of weakness. I've learned that some of us will have to suffer publicly for the millions who suffer silently. They are chosen to tell their story so others can know that they are not alone, and find the strength and courage to face their fears. For most people, it is easier to blend in than stand out. They cannot be blamed for that as the world can be a cruel and harsh place. We are told to speak our truth, and then we are judged for it. However, nothing is more liberating than when we free ourselves of the opinions and criticisms of others. We will be judged, condemned and criticized anyway, might as well let it be for being you!

I've lived under every political system, and I've learned that no matter how differently we view the world, we are all just curious beings trying to survive on this harsh, yet beautiful planet.

Sometimes circumstances cause us to live far away from home, but while our spirit may roam, we cannot deceive our hearts. Home is always where the heart is. I've learned that sometimes we may stray from ourselves hoping it will please others and make us happy, but our true selves cannot be denied and we will eventually find our way back. Growing up on an island and coming from humble beginnings, I was told in many ways that I was not good enough and was destined for failure. I was supposed to be a high school dropout, pregnant, ignorant, and all the other labels that come with the stereotypes of a girl like me. Nonetheless, I always believed in myself and remained a curious butterfly.

My imagination allowed me to envision a life greater than what would have been expected for a girl like me. I wanted to see the world and everything in it, and I did! This dream seemed unattainable because of my circumstances, but I always knew deep down that God had a greater plan for my life. Throughout my journey, I was searching for my own voice, and the more I learned, the more I felt connected to all the girls like me who often feel trapped and simply wants their voices to be heard. Many who knew of me and my story, wanted to have the "Cinderella" life also. I felt a huge responsibility to live up to that ideal, all while wanting to scream out, "there is no Cinderella story! Everything in life requires hard work and great compromise!" It's important that one knows their worth and a have a sense of identity before attempting to make anyone else happy. We can add to people's happiness, but we are responsible for our own happiness, and we can only be happy when we stay true to our authentic self. I urge young women everywhere to have their own lives, before becoming anybody's wife.

As a teenager, I got the opportunity to move to the United States and have a more affluent lifestyle. I thought that finally all my dreams would come true and I would be happy. I quickly learned that sometimes less is more. Of all the fascinating places I've seen, and all the things I've acquired, the most valuable has been my education. It's something that lives within me which no can ever take away. When I got all the things that I thought would define me and make me happy, I found out that I was already happy without them. I had everything I needed. A family who loved me and was always there for me and a mother who led by example and instilled the right values and discipline within us so we could grow into strong men and women of character and conviction. We were not rich, but we understood the true value of family and even when we drifted apart, we always found our way back to each other. Our bond is one that cannot be broken and throughout my journey, I truly realized the importance and true meaning of family.

Along the way I met people that have enhanced and enriched my world with their character and leadership. There were some lessons I learned the hard way, but it caused me to focus on the girl in the mirror and know that change starts with me. I am always a work in progress, and whenever I feel like my work is done, God sends me a reminder that I am not without sin or flaws, and I have to keep working on me. I continue to surround myself with people who bring out the best in me and inspire me to do better. The journey of discovering one's true self can be a long and arduous one, but I've learned that if we are willing to face our fears and learn from every experience--- good and bad, then we can tap into our greatness and grow into the person we want and choose to become. Life is beautiful, and I continue to embrace it with open arms.

Made in the USA
Columbia, SC
14 February 2018